PRAISE FOR

A SHORT HISTORY OF PRESIDENTIAL ELECTION CRISES

"Hirsch does a very good job of offering historical context to illuminate the present—and the terrifying future. His imaginative proposals are probably too sensible to be implemented in an age of parochial partisanship."
— David Shipler, Pulitzer Prize–winning former reporter for the *New York Times*

"Democracy is broken, but as Alan Hirsch explains, it really doesn't have to be. This is the real story of how our voting system became so vulnerable to attacks from within and without, told with precision, verve, and even hope. This is the way out."
— Douglas Rushkoff, author of *Team Human*

"This is a must-read for anyone who cares about safeguarding presidential elections—which should be everyone. Alan Hirsch illuminates and captivates as he unpacks our history of close and chaotic presidential elections occasioned by the Electoral College, and he masterfully develops the case for shifting to a national popular election. He then addresses contemporary technological threats to electoral legitimacy such as hacked elections or suppressed turnout, and offers a novel and provocative political (and, dare one say, nonpartisan) solution. The time to read this book and pay attention is now."
— Evan Caminker, Professor and former Dean, University of Michigan Law School

"Incredibly readable, well-researched, analytically sound and important."

—Alan B. Morrison, Associate Dean for Public Interest & Public Service at the George Washington Law School

"As the producer of *The Forum* in San Francisco, which strives to foster civil conversation on complex issues, I couldn't have asked for a more mature, sophisticated, and fair look at impeachment, as Alan Hirsch provides in *Impeaching the President: Past, Present, and Future*. I can't tell you how reassuring it is to find an adult voice on this issue, calmly and clearly breaking through all of the current bombast and posturing. Everyone who is concerned about the governance of our country should read this book."

—Rebecca Nestle, Director of Cultural Programs, Grace Cathedral

"Absolutely enjoyed this one. The reader gets a hearty mix of American history, political intrigue, and constitutional law, all adhered with Hirsch's amazing writing. He captures the political chaos surrounding each prior case, yanking the reader out of our present exceptionalism to see the evolution of impeachment with the proper context and clarity. We have been here before and will likely be here again many more times, he suggests, with increased frequency. Can't recommend it enough."

—Travis Cohen, Brookline Booksmith

A Short History of Presidential Election Crises

(and how to prevent the next one)

Alan Hirsch

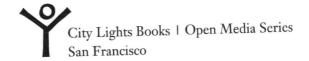

City Lights Books | Open Media Series
San Francisco

Copyright 2020 © by Alan Hirsch

All Rights Reserved.

Cover design by: Herb Thornby

Open Media Series Editor: Greg Ruggiero

ISBN: 978-0-87286-829-8

Library of Congress Cataloging-in-Publication Data
Names: Hirsch, Alan, 1959- author.
Title: A short history of presidential election crises : (and how to prevent the next one) / Alan Hirsch.
Description: San Francisco, CA : City Lights Books, 2020. | Series: Open Media series | Includes bibliographical references.
Identifiers: LCCN 2019054933 | ISBN 9780872868298 (trade paperback)
Subjects: LCSH: Presidents—United States—Election—History. | Elections—Security measures—United States. | Electoral college—United States.
Classification: LCC JK524 .H57 2020 | DDC 324.973—dc23
LC record available at https://lccn.loc.gov/2019054933

City Lights Books are published at the City Lights Bookstore
261 Columbus Avenue, San Francisco, CA 94133
www.citylights.com

CONTENTS

INTRODUCTION

While the Russian government engaged in covert operations in order to influence the 2016 United States presidential election, no evidence indicates any direct alteration of the vote tabulation—for example, converting votes for Hillary Clinton to votes for Donald Trump. But suppose someone does hack voting machines, and those efforts decide the outcome of the election. What mechanism in the Constitution enables us to reverse an illegitimate election?

You may be surprised to learn the answer: There is none. The U.S. Constitution provides no means for undoing an illegitimate presidential election. Article II sets forth procedures for electing the president, but does nothing to ensure the legitimacy of the outcome. In the more than two centuries since the Constitution was ratified, neither Congress nor the states have filled the void. Today, in the age of hacking, the continued failure to act would be stunningly shortsighted.

The problem transcends improper interference with an election. Outright cheating—the stuffing of ballot boxes, dead people voting, hacking, and other species of fraud—is not the only way an election can go awry. Even in a relatively honest competition, circumstances may render it difficult to determine the actual winner. Just ask Al Gore. The monthlong chaos and convoluted litigation that ensued in Florida after the votes were tallied in 2000 reflected the absence of a reliable procedure for resolving a disputed election.

To some extent, the 2000 nightmare stemmed from a perverse alignment of the stars, a series of circumstances that will never be replicated. (Among other things, the election came down to the state that happened to be governed by the brother of one of the candidates.) But it would be a mistake to think that only a fluke can create a presidential election crisis. The year 2000 was the fourth time—along with 1800, 1824, and 1876—that a presidential election left the nation with no clear winner and no reliable process for determining one. Many other elections (1880, 1888, 1916, 1960, 1968, 1976, 2004, and 2016) were sufficiently close that a malfunction or misfeasance in a few states could have affected the outcome. All told, in *twelve* presidential elections, more than 20 percent of all such contests, the result was too close for comfort.

This is no accident. Rather, it stems from America's unusual method of picking a president. We often hear attacks on the Electoral College because of its undemocratic nature: Someone can become president despite receiving millions fewer votes than his or her opponent. Equally troubling aspects of the Electoral College, however, have gone overlooked, including its capacity to produce cliff-hanger elections. In addition, the Electoral College may have been introduced to reinforce white supremacy.

Our flawed method of choosing a president calls to mind Charles Dudley Warner's quip about the weather: Everyone talks about it, but no one does anything about it. It is remarkable that, notwithstanding several crisis-ridden presidential elections, we have done little to remedy the underlying problems. In the aftermath of the first crisis election, in 1800, Congress did pass and the states then ratified the Twelfth Amendment to the Constitution, a partially successful effort to prevent a recurrence. The same cannot be said for the response to later disasters. No reforms followed the 1824 train wreck of an election. Fortunately, it took a half century before the nation experienced another dangerously uncertain presidential election. After the 1876 fiasco, in which the outcome was determined by a partisan commission and backroom dealing, we might have expected remedial action. Congress passed one relevant statute, but it was wholly inadequate. This time, though, the nation proved luckier. It took more than a century for another full-bore crisis. After the imbroglio in 2000, just as after the crisis-ridden elections of 1824 and 1876, little was done to prevent a recurrence.

That is not to say that our method of choosing

a president has remained the same. In the nation's early days, members of the Electoral College were selected by state legislatures. Today, virtually every state picks its electors through a statewide popular vote. The Twelfth Amendment enables the presidential and vice presidential candidates of each party to run as a unified ticket. The Fourteenth Amendment stipulates that any state that denies African Americans the vote will receive a reduced number of electoral votes, and the Twenty-Third Amendment gives the District of Columbia electoral votes. None of these changes, however, does anything to prevent the kinds of crises that have arisen on multiple occasions. We remain vulnerable to another crisis. Indeed, in the age of hacking, we are more vulnerable than ever.

This book is motivated by a combination of three circumstances. First, history teaches that we often experience razor-close presidential elections, which can and sometimes do produce crises. Second, our method of picking the president invites serious problems, and new circumstances have increased the risk. Third, we lack the means of resolving the next crisis, even though we have every reason to fear one.

The implicit premise of this book is the philosopher George Santayana's oft-cited maxim that the failure to learn from history assures repeating its mistakes. With that in mind, the first five chapters revisit the controversial elections of 1800, 1824, 1876, 2000, and 2016. This journey tees up Chapters Six and Seven, which propose

constitutional amendments designed to prevent recur-
rences. Chapter Six advocates an amendment that would
reduce the likelihood of elections producing a crisis, and
Chapter Seven proposes an amendment that would establish a rational procedure for resolving the crises that
do arise.

ONE

EARLY ELECTIONS

Elections are the lifeblood of a republic, and the election of the president, the nation's most powerful public official, loomed largest for the Founding Fathers. The delegates who gathered in Philadelphia in 1787 for the Constitutional Convention discussed at length the process of electing the president—the issue came up on twenty-one different days and occasioned thirty separate votes.[1] *The Federalist*, the influential collection of essays promoting ratification of the Constitution, addresses presidential elections in eight different essays, one of which (*Federalist* 68, by Alexander Hamilton) deals with it exclusively. Yet, for all that attention, the Constitution produced a mode of election that amounted to an accident waiting to happen—and the wait wasn't long.

How could the framers get something so important so wrong? The answer, in a word, is parties. Or their absence. Political parties played little role in the framers' thinking, because they didn't yet exist. Before long, however, they sprang up and dominated the political landscape. Absent parties, the Constitution's mechanism for electing the president made at least some sense. Each state, in proportion to its population, would get a certain number of "electors"—the only people to cast ballots for president (with each state to determine how its electors would be selected). Each elector would cast *two* votes for president. The person receiving a majority of the electoral votes would become president; the runner-up would become vice president. Why not? A next-in-command is needed in case the president dies or otherwise leaves office, and who better than the person the voters hold in second-highest esteem?

To be sure, such a system would make no sense today. In 2016, it could have resulted in President Trump and Vice President Clinton, a rather infelicitous partnership. But at the nation's creation, electors were not deciding between candidates from different parties after a competitive election. In fact, there were no candidates, no parties, and no competition. No one *ran* for president or even declared interest. The electors were simply expected to decide who would be the best man for the job. The second best person—the one receiving the second-highest number of votes—would become vice president. In the event no one received a majority of the electoral votes, the House of Representatives would choose the president.

This system worked reasonably well for the nation's first two elections. In 1788, the sixty-nine electors unanimously voted in George Washington; thirty-four of the sixty-nine tapped John Adams with their other vote, easily surpassing the total (nine) of the third-place finisher, John Jay. It had always been assumed that the first president would be Washington, the Revolutionary War hero who presided over the Constitutional Convention. To no one's surprise, the second slot fell to Adams, the most important nonmilitary figure in the American Revolution. With the notable exception of the prickly Adams himself, who expressed bitterness that so many electors declined to support him, virtually everyone approved the result. The nation thus began with President Washington and Vice President Adams, a talented and public-spirited duo. They were re-elected in 1792, Washington again unanimously and Adams this time receiving the votes of seventy-seven of the 132 electors.

The broadly approved outcome of the first two elections masked two potential problems. First, what if all the electors had cast one ballot each for Washington and Adams? Under that plausible scenario, there would have been a tie for the presidency, throwing the election to the House. Foreseeing this possibility—or, worse, a few quirky electors omitting Washington, and Adams ending up president—Alexander Hamilton lobbied some electors not to vote for Adams, so as to ensure Washington's election to the top spot. But apart from Hamilton, who privately noted this "defect in the Constitution,"[2] few worried about a tie, perhaps because such an occurrence would have been easily resolved: The House would have elected Washington president and Adams vice president. Not even Adams would have expected otherwise or protested the result.

So too, no one raised the risk of a second troubling scenario: What if the men to finish first and second were adversaries, leaving the president saddled with an antagonistic "partner" in office? (Adams was actually the rare Founder not enamored of Washington, but for the most part he kept his misgivings to himself.) But this problem, too, seems magnified through the prism of political parties. Absent such parties, the antagonism between president and vice president would be personal only, a circumstance that could be transcended through maturity and good will.

Thus, if the original method of selecting the president and vice president created the seeds of crisis because of a potential tie or a schizophrenic "team," neither problem seemed likely to arise. But both would before long.

By the time Washington stepped down after two terms, political parties were clearly established. Adams and Hamilton led the incumbent party, the Federalists; Thomas Jefferson and James Madison led the opposition, the Democratic-Republicans (or Republicans for short). The bitter divide between these parties produced the first contested presidential election, in 1796. While it remained the case that no one formally declared their candidacy or campaigned openly, everyone understood Adams and Jefferson to be the respective choices of the Federalists and Republicans. South Carolina's Thomas

Pinckney served as Adams's de facto running mate, while Aaron Burr was Jefferson's. Such designations were unofficial, and the voting mechanism remained the same: each elector would cast two votes for president (none for vice president) and the second-place finisher would become vice president.

Adams prevailed in a tight election, receiving seventy-one electoral votes to Jefferson's sixty-eight. Some scheming produced ticket-splitting, such that Pinckney received only fifty-nine votes and Burr just thirty. The result was that, while Adams won the presidency, Jefferson, rather than Adams's running mate Pinckney, was elected vice president. The Adams-Jefferson administration consisted of a president and vice president from different parties. And though they had been co-revolutionaries and close friends, Adams and Jefferson differed markedly in their political philosophies. Indeed, ten months prior to the election, in a letter to his wife, Abigail, Adams prophesied that he and Jefferson as president/vice president (in either order) would produce a "dangerous crisis in public affairs" because the two were in "opposite boxes."[3]

For the first time, the Constitution's mechanism for electing the president and vice president had proven problematic, producing an administration potentially at war with itself. "The Lion & the Lamb are to lie down together," observed Hamilton, who detested both lion and lamb (Adams and Jefferson). "Sceptics like me quietly look forward to the event—willing to hope but not prepared to believe."[4]

Some Federalists were more pessimistic and looked to prevent a recurrence of the lion/lamb problem that resulted from electors voting only for president. They proposed constitutional amendments that would require electors to vote separately for president and vice president, which would actually make it easier to elect a united administration. The proposals went nowhere, but the concern that triggered them proved justified: Over the next four years, Vice President Jefferson opposed (with various degrees of openness) many of the policies of President Adams.[5]

The resistance of his own vice president proved a headache for Adams, but not an existential threat to the nation. The Adams-Jefferson intra-administration discord paled in comparison to the crisis created by the next presidential election, in 1800. In that rematch between Adams and Jefferson, the Constitution's flawed process produced the other potentially catastrophic scenario that the framers had inadvertently made likely: a tie. Not a tie between the parties' respective presidential candidates, but rather a tie between one of them (Jefferson) and his running mate (Burr).

As in 1796, it was understood that Jefferson was the presidential candidate and Burr his junior partner, but there remained no mechanism for electors to distinguish between their two choices. Rather, as before, they cast two votes for president (and none for vice president). In 1796, many Republican electors had voted for Jefferson but not Burr. That changed in 1800, because Republicans learned from the Federalists' mistake. Recall that in 1796 twelve Federalist electors did not use their second vote on Adams's running mate Pinckney, allowing Jefferson to sneak in to the vice presidency. In 1800, every Republican elector cast one vote for Jefferson and one for Burr, giving them seventy-three electoral votes each. Adams received sixty-five, and his unofficial running mate, Charles Pinckney (cousin of his previous running mate, Thomas), sixty-four. One Federalist elector was smart enough to vote for someone other than Pinckney and thus avert a tie in the event the Federalists won. There was talk of a few Republican electors doing the same. However, because of concern that too many electors would do so, thereby allowing Adams to secure the second spot, none did. Republicans *over-learned* the lesson of 1796. Professor Akhil Amar succinctly captures the result: "Even though almost all Republicans electors had in their minds voted for Jefferson first and Burr second, on the formal paper ballots these two candidates emerged as equals."[6]

Recall our speculation that a tie between Washington and Adams would have been unproblematic: The House of Representatives would have elected Washington president without much fuss. Ideally, the Jefferson-Burr tie would have produced a similarly uncontroversial result. After all, no one doubted that Jefferson was the top of the ticket, the man the Republican electors wished to make president.

But the combination of two circumstances prevented the easy resolution: 1) Aaron Burr was a conniver who wanted to be president; and 2) Federalists wanted anyone but Jefferson as president. They calculated that the notoriously nonideological Burr would work with them if he were indebted to them. Burr did nothing to discourage such calculations, declining to renounce interest in the top spot.

The Constitution dictates that, when a presidential election is thrown to the House, the voting goes state by state, with each state receiving one vote, and a majority of the states needed for victory. On the first ballot, eight states tapped Jefferson and six chose Burr, while Vermont and Maryland deadlocked. (Every Federalist representative voted for Burr.) That left Jefferson one short of the nine states needed for victory. One week and thirty-five ballots later, the stalemate remained—despite extensive backroom maneuvering, including efforts by the Federalists to extract promises from Jefferson in exchange for their votes. Alexander Hamilton, a leading Federalist and enemy of both Jefferson and Burr, let it be known that he regarded Jefferson as the lesser of the two evils. Even so, as the March 4 date for the president's inauguration rapidly approached, there was a real prospect of the nation without a leader.

Before the thirty-sixth ballot, however, James Bayard, Delaware's sole representative, announced that he would switch from Burr to Jefferson to end the crisis. Bayard ended up abstaining instead, leaving Delaware in neither candidate's column. However, a few Federalist

House members from Maryland and Vermont who previously supported Burr followed Bayard's lead and abstained. That gave Jefferson those states, and ten states total, breaking the deadlock and averting disaster.

The election of 1800 belied Alexander Hamilton's confident claim that the Constitution set forth a method of selecting the president that safeguarded against "tumult and disorder."[7] But the Founders knew a constitutional crisis when they saw one, and looked to amend the Constitution to prevent a recurrence. The Twelfth Amendment was proposed in December 1803 and ratified in June 1804, in time to govern the 1804 election. The amendment is roughly 370 words (a page and a half, typed), much of it confusing or peripheral. But it did the heavy lifting in a few sentences: "[The electors] shall name in their ballots the person voted for as President, and in distinct ballots the person voted for as Vice-President. . . . The person having the greatest number of votes for President shall be the President, if such number be a majority of the whole number of electors appointed. . . . The person having the greatest number of votes as Vice-President, shall be the Vice-President."

By separating the votes for president and vice president, the amendment promised to avert repeats of the untoward scenarios from the two previous elections. It would now be possible for a party's presidential and vice presidential nominees effectively to run as a ticket, without fear of them ending up tied for president, à la 1800, and without someone from the opposing party sneaking in to become vice president, à la 1796.

It worked as planned in 1804. The 162 electors who voted for Jefferson for president cast a separate ballot for his running mate, Governor George Clinton, for vice president. Unlike in 1800, when Burr received presidential votes along with Jefferson, Clinton received no presidential votes: no inadvertent tie, no crisis in the House. And unlike 1796, when Jefferson and Adams were forced together into a schizophrenic administration, now Jefferson and his vice president served harmoniously.

Unfortunately, while the Twelfth Amendment prevented repeats of the 1796 and 1800 fiascos, its drafters failed to anticipate other ways in which a presidential election might go off the rails. Just twenty years later, the election of 1824 produced another constitutional crisis. The problem stemmed from the provision that, if no candidate receives a majority of the electoral votes, the president shall be determined by the House of Representatives. To be sure, that provision also contributed to the crisis in 1800, but for a different reason: In 1824, the failure of any candidate to receive a majority resulted not from a tie but rather from a multicandidate field—four candidates with significant support.

When it comes to the scenario in which no candidate receives a majority of the electoral votes, the Twelfth Amendment simply imported the language of the original Constitution (apart from one tweak, noted next chapter). Accordingly, the possibility of a deadlocked House, and all the mischief and chicanery that could bring, remained. In 1824, the nation paid the price for that provision: When none of the four candidates received a majority of electoral votes, the election went to the House, where it was eventually resolved in a fashion so dangerous that it risked fomenting rebellion.

ELECTION OF 1824

James Monroe served as president from 1816 to 1824, a period misleadingly termed the "Era of Good Feeling." It was actually a time of considerable national contentiousness over, among other things, the treatment of Native Americans, slavery, a national bank, and tariffs. Despite the fractiousness, Monroe was easily elected and re-elected president. In 1816, he received 183 out of the 217 electoral votes. More impressive, in 1820 he received all but one of the 232 electoral votes. (For some reason, one elector opted for John Quincy Adams, Monroe's secretary of state.)

Monroe's electoral dominance stemmed from the absence of significant opposition. The Federalists, considerably weakened during the Jefferson administration, slowly withered away as a national force following the War of 1812. Any "good feeling" in the period thereafter resulted from the absence of competing parties. Monroe's near-unanimous victory in 1820 echoed George Washington's, but with a major difference. When Washington was elected unanimously in 1788, there were no parties. Now there was *one*: the Republicans. Hence Monroe's coronation.

But politics abhors a vacuum. With Monroe poised to follow the precedent established by Washington and step down after his second term, every prominent politician could see himself in the White House. The year 1824 promised to be the opposite of 1820: the one-man "race" replaced by a multicandidate scrum. The names of at least seventeen potential candidates were bandied about.

No matter who prevailed, the election would witness a generational passing of the torch. Unlike his would-be successors, Monroe was a Founding Father—he fought in the Revolutionary War, served in the Continental Congress, was elected to the U.S. Senate in 1790, and was appointed secretary of state by President James Madison. As a matter of political and historical logic, it made sense for him to pass the baton to his secretary of state, John Quincy Adams. The position of secretary of state had become the standard stepping stone—Jefferson, Madison, and Monroe had all served in that position before becoming president. Moreover, Adams was literally a second-generation Founder—the oldest son of America's first vice president and second president, John Adams.

By virtue of upbringing, experience, and intellect, John Quincy Adams was probably the most qualified person ever to seek the presidency. As a toddler, he accompanied his father around Europe during the latter's diplomatic missions. A standout student at Harvard who built a promising legal practice, Adams was just twenty-seven when George Washington appointed him minister to Prussia in 1794. In 1803, he was chosen U.S. senator from Massachusetts. Young Adams shared his father's disdain for political parties, including their own Federalist Party. His mutual antipathy with leading Federalists led to his resignation from the Senate in 1808. He then briefly became a Harvard professor, but left the post when named minister to Russia by President Madison in 1809. He stayed in that position for five years, before Madison appointed him to the commission that negotiated the Treaty of Ghent to end the War of 1812. Adams was subsequently appointed secretary of state by President Monroe in 1817, and formulated the Monroe Doctrine opposing European colonialism in the Americas.

If Adams's credentials were unimpeachable, the same could not be said for his personality and temperament. Even friends found him aloof; he made little effort to conceal his sense of superiority. Adams also inherited his father's thin skin. As the presidential pre-campaign heated up in the winter of 1822, he complained that "no man in America has made his way through showers of ribaldry and invective . . . more frequent and various than I have breasted."[8]

This personal prickliness dovetailed with a political problem: He was virtually a man without a party. The remnants of the Federalists considered him an apostate. He effectively switched to the Republicans (now the only national party), but they regarded him as a

Johnny-come-lately. Despite his impeccable qualifications, in the early stages of the 1824 election, Adams was not considered the front-runner.

That designation belonged to Monroe's secretary of the treasury, William Crawford, a native-born Virginian (though his parents moved to South Carolina and later Georgia when he was young). Crawford's election as president would have continued the Virginia dynasty— for thirty-one of the nation's first thirty-five years, a Virginian occupied the president's seat. He shared not only George Washington's home state, but also his imposing physique, standing six foot three and weighing more than two hundred pounds. A states-rights Republican, the hot-tempered Crawford participated in two duels, killing a man in 1802 and suffering a severe wound in 1806. But that hardly distinguished him in this field. Three of the five major candidates (Andrew Jackson and Henry Clay as well as Crawford) had fought in duels. Remarkably, at the time duels were widely considered an acceptable means of dispute resolution.

The less bloody part of Crawford's impressive résumé included a term in the U.S. Senate followed by service in several prominent positions in the Madison administration: minister to France during the War of 1812, secretary of war, and secretary of the treasury. Supporters urged Crawford to pursue the presidency in 1816, but he deferred to Monroe—and nevertheless came in a close second for the Republican Party's nomination. Monroe kept Crawford on at the Department of the Treasury, where he "sat serenely . . . awaiting his turn at the Presidency with every assurance of success, only to be suddenly surprised by the appearance in the field of a swarm of candidates."[9]

One of those candidates, another perceived powerhouse and member of Monroe's cabinet, was John C. Calhoun. The South Carolinian prodigy went north for education at the finest schools—Yale and Judge Tapping Reeve's famous Litchfield Law School in Connecticut—before returning to South Carolina and establishing a successful law practice. Calhoun was elected to the state legislature at the age of twenty-six in 1808 and to the U.S. House two years later. The anti-British war hawk achieved prominence by pushing for the War of 1812. He ran unopposed for Congress in 1812 and 1814 and was appointed secretary of war by Monroe in 1817. In December 1821, Calhoun formally accepted the invitation of several congressmen to announce his interest in the presidency, becoming the first in the field to declare.

Although he would later acquire notoriety for advocating for the South's secession from the Union, in the early 1820s Calhoun preached no such heresies. On the contrary, Adams pronounced him "above all sectional and factious prejudices more than any other statesman of the Union with whom I have ever acted."[10] In Congress, Calhoun had been a stalwart supporter of the second national bank, and as secretary of war, he strengthened the U.S. Army. In 1824, Calhoun was a distinctly national, rather than regional, candidate.

Adams, Crawford, and Calhoun, all prominent members of Monroe's cabinet, were joined as presidential candidates by Henry Clay and Andrew Jackson. Like Crawford, Clay was born in Virginia but raised elsewhere in the South (in his case, Kentucky). Like Adams and Calhoun, he became an accomplished lawyer before turning to politics. Clay was elected to the Kentucky state legislature in 1803, appointed to the U.S. Senate in 1806 and 1809 to fill unexpired terms, then elected to the House in 1810 and immediately made Speaker. Like Calhoun, he pushed for U.S. entry into the War of 1812, and like Adams, he accepted President Madison's appointment to the commission that negotiated the Treaty of Ghent. But Clay rebuffed Madison's effort to join his cabinet, remaining until 1820 in the House, where he crafted the Missouri Compromise of 1820 and established himself as a leading critic of the Monroe administration.

Financial problems led Clay to resign his seat rather than seek re-election in 1820; he took a more lucrative position as attorney for the Bank of the U.S. in the West. But he again ran for the House in 1822, was elected, and was again chosen Speaker. As cheerful as Adams was dour, Clay was a charismatic orator and powerhouse Speaker of the House. He managed to be both a voice for the West and a militant nationalist, a lifelong advocate of an economic program termed the "American System," which combined protective tariffs, transportation development, and a national bank.

General Andrew Jackson, the sole veteran in the

field of candidates, was a veritable war hero. Eventually it would become commonplace for soldiers to use their experience as a stepping stone to politics (William Henry Harrison, Zachary Taylor, Ulysses S. Grant, Rutherford B. Hayes, Theodore Roosevelt, Dwight D. Eisenhower, and John F. Kennedy all rode their military exploits to the White House), but Jackson was the first presidential candidate since George Washington with a background on the battlefield rather than traditional political experience. Jackson's warrior days began young, when he skirmished against the British as a thirteen-year-old boy. He was captured and allegedly wounded when he refused to clean a British officer's boots. Such a beginning fits with Jackson's defiant personality. His father died before he was born, and his mother while he was a teen. The unrestrained orphan lived large and dangerously.

Trained as an attorney, as were all the major presidential candidates, Jackson became a successful prosecutor in his home state of Tennessee. He was elected to the U.S. House of Representatives in 1796, and shortly thereafter selected to fill a Senate vacancy (when his ally William Blount was expelled for conspiring with Great Britain). Jackson, who disliked the Senate, resigned and returned home in 1798. He was almost immediately elected judge on the state superior court and in 1802 was appointed a major-general in the Tennessee militia. Jackson retired as a judge in 1803, but remained a militia leader, leading to his appointment as a major-general in the U.S. Army. His victory over the British in the Battle of New Orleans in January 1815, the last major battle of the War of 1812, furthered his reputation as a warrior. In 1823, a group of his supporters—the so-called "Nashville Junto"—helped get him elected to the U.S. Senate, which they saw as his path to the presidency. Jackson was a slaveholder and unabashed white supremacist, and his military exploits included tremendous violence against Native Americans, but to the white male electorate in 1824, these were not necessarily disadvantages.

The quintet of top-shelf candidates—Adams, Crawford, Calhoun, Clay, and Jackson—ensured the breaking of at least one presidential streak. By 1824, the White House had been occupied by Virginians for twenty-four consecutive years, and the last three presidents had previously served as secretary of state. Adams, the only present or former secretary of state in contention, hailed from Massachusetts.

Each of the five candidates had a plausible path to the presidency. Calhoun, Crawford, and Adams, major figures in the popular Monroe administration, could each be seen as a logical successor. (Monroe maintained an official neutrality, but was suspected of pulling strings behind the scenes to help Calhoun.) Clay, for his part, needed only to finish in the top three, provided that no one receive a majority of the electoral votes. The election would then be thrown to the House of Representatives, where he, the Speaker, would be the overwhelming favorite. In his diary, John Quincy Adams noted rumors that Clay had come out of retirement to reclaim his position as Speaker precisely as "a step for his own promotion to the Presidency on the very probable contingency that the election would fall to the House of Representatives."[11] Meanwhile, the war hero Jackson enjoyed the greatest popularity with ordinary Americans, and benefited from the kind of grass-roots campaign that was at the time uncommon in America.

In the latter part of the twentieth century, there would be much reference to the "endless campaign" or "perpetual campaign" for president. As it happens, the phenomenon of the next presidential election starting virtually as soon as the previous one concludes goes way back. In January 1822, with Monroe's second term less than a year old, the political writer Hezekiah Niles lamented the excessive time spent by politicians and others "in electioneering for the next President of the United States."[12] A few months later, another journalist noted that the "electioneering begins to wax hot."[13]

The election of 1824 was, in a sense, the first modern presidential election, replete with campaign biographies, straw polls, and other campaign accoutrements that would eventually become commonplace. Many state legislatures held conventions that drafted resolutions endorsing a candidate. On February 14, 1824, the U.S. Congress held its quadrennial "caucus" to anoint its own candidate. This had become the traditional means for Republicans to select their nominee, but in 1824 the caucus came under heavy criticism for bypassing the people at large. As a result, all but Crawford's supporters (and even some of them) boycotted the caucus. Crawford received sixty-two of the sixty-six votes cast, but this Valentine's Day massacre may actually have harmed his candidacy, since Crawford was tarred as the beneficiary of an elitist cabal. A Jackson supporter from Pennsylvania expressed a widespread sentiment when he attacked the caucus as a game played by "the friends of a single individual, held in utter disregard or defiance of the known wishes of the Democratic Party in Congress and throughout the Union."[14]

Five months earlier, in September 1823, Crawford had suffered a greater blow—a stroke that left him paralyzed and blind. However, he gradually recovered mobility and vision in the months ahead without the public ever learning about the seriousness of his condition, and he remained in the race until the end. (He survived for a full decade after the election.) If the truth about Crawford's extreme condition failed to derail his candidacy, the inverse occurred with Clay: False rumors of ill health fueled speculation that he had dropped out of the race, and thus significantly impeded his candidacy. Clay would later blame his defeat on "fabrications of tales of my withdrawal."[15]

Despite their struggles, Crawford and Clay survived as major candidates—unlike Calhoun. When some of his strongest supporters defected to Jackson in early 1824, Calhoun could see the writing on the wall and made known his intention to seek the vice presidency instead of the top spot.

With Calhoun out and Clay and Crawford suffering

serious setbacks, Jackson and Adams pulled ahead in the final months. When the votes were counted on December 6, 1824, Jackson received 152,901, or 41 percent of all votes cast; Adams received 114,023 (31 percent); Clay 47,217 (13 percent); and Crawford 46,979 (13 percent). The Electoral College vote tracked the popular vote reasonably closely, though Clay and Crawford swapped positions. Jackson received the votes of ninety-nine electors Adams eighty-four, Crawford forty-one, and Clay thirty-seven.

Jackson fell thirty-two electoral votes short of a majority, and thus the election was thrown to the House of Representatives. Under the Twelfth Amendment to the Constitution, the House would choose among the top three candidates. Under the original Constitution, it had been the top five, and that tweak changed history. Although Clay received more popular votes than Crawford, he received four fewer electoral votes, knocking him out of consideration and thwarting his strategy of prevailing in the House. The House would choose among Jackson, Adams, and Crawford, with Clay relegated to the role of power broker.

The dangers of such a "contingent" election in the House, in which each state gets one vote, had been prophesied in 1823 by Thomas Jefferson. In a letter to a friend, written just 14 months before the 1824 election, the aged Jefferson said that he had long regarded the process of the House selecting the president if no one received a majority of electoral votes "the most dangerous blot on our Constitution, and one which some unlucky chance will someday hit."[16] Jefferson meant hit *again*. No one knew better than he that the House selecting the President, with all the chicanery that would invite, had already occurred—in 1800, when, despite everyone knowing that the electors intended for Jefferson (and not Aaron Burr) to be President, it took thirty-six ballots and some backroom dealing to produce that result. Now, just twenty-four years later, the nation again faced the prospect of a covert post-election campaign.

While the presidential vote produced potential chaos, the vice presidential tally proved smooth and painless. With a de facto one-party system in effect, there were no president–vice president tickets in 1824. The electors, casting their ballots for vice president without any link to the presidency, overwhelmingly chose Calhoun. He received 182 electoral votes, and no one else more than thirty. Oddly, Calhoun would be re-elected vice president in 1828 even as a new man was elected president. Calhoun was one of just two men in American history to serve as vice president under two presidents. (George Clinton served under Jefferson and Madison.) Given his controversial views and outsize personality, Calhoun does not seem like the vice-presidential type, but history cast him in that role.

On February 9, 1825, the House met to select the president, just as it had done during the election of 1800. But now, with the country more populated, the structural oddity of the process by which the House made its choice was more apparent. Once again, in keeping with the Constitution, each state received one vote. Accordingly, the single congressman from tiny Delaware wielded as much power as New York's thirty-four representatives. But a single congressman from Kentucky was widely presumed to have the power to determine the next president. Now that he was out of the running, Clay could sway the House to elect Jackson, Adams, or Crawford. Clay was believed to control the House members representing the four states that he had won in November, and perhaps to have influence over others as well. As one Adams supporter observed, either ruefully or hopefully, it was "very much in Clay's power to make the President."[17]

Surrogates of the three remaining candidates aggressively courted Clay. Hypocrisy flourished, as men who had attacked the Speaker for months suddenly discovered his virtues. Clay professed to find the notion that he controlled the House strings "very amusing" and quipped that "the friends of all the three gentlemen are so very courteous, and affectionate, that I sometimes almost wish that it was in my power to accommodate each of them."[18] But Clay scoffed at the prospect of selling his services in exchange for a cabinet position: "I would not cross Pennsylvania Avenue to be in any office under any Administration which lies before us."[19] So he said on December 22, 1824. Maybe he dissembled, maybe he later changed his mind.

Clay never seriously considered supporting Crawford, if only because of the latter's ill health. From the beginning Clay confided to friends that, if he indeed were the power broker, Adams or Jackson would be the beneficiary. He regarded this choice as the lesser of two evils. "Most probably it will be either Genl. Jackson or Mr. Adams," Clay wrote a friend on December 13. "And what an alternative that is!"[20]

Jackson and Clay never got along. By contrast, Adams and Clay had enjoyed a cordial relationship. They had served together on the commission that negotiated the Treaty of Ghent in 1815, and later, when Clay was Speaker of the House and Adams secretary of state, they worked together on various affairs of state and occasionally dined together. But early in 1822 their relationship soured over a pamphlet written by a Clay supporter who served with both men on the Ghent commission. The pamphlet alleged that Adams sought favorable terms for Great Britain in those negotiations in exchange for benefits to New England fisheries. Adams believed Clay responsible for the pamphlet; Clay angrily denied the charge.

Clay considered Jackson a crude warrior unschooled in legislation and negotiation— Clay's life work. The only case to be made for supporting Jackson was that he was the closest thing to the people's choice, having received the most popular and electoral votes. Such consideration could not overcome Clay's wholesale contempt for Jackson, whose election, Clay surmised, would "give to the Military Spirit a Stimulus and a confidence that might lead to the most pernicious results."[21]

Adams had Clay's respect but not affection, which is

pretty much how everyone felt about Adams. From the time of the November election until the House vote in February, Clay hinted to friends that he preferred Adams to Jackson. Sometimes he did more than hint. For example, in a letter to a friend dated December 28, Clay stated that "I have no hesitation in saying that I have long since decided in favor of Mr. Adams."[22] However, he did not make that preference public.

As the date for the House to decide grew nearer, Clay dropped the pretense that he lacked the power to determine the winner or to benefit personally from doing so. In a letter dated January 23, 1825, he stated that "my friends have probably the power of controlling the ultimate result" and, as for the prospect of him securing a cabinet position, "I believe that, if I choose to go into it, I can enter in *any* situation that I may please."[23] Clay's dealmaking was a source of constant speculation. Congressman James Buchanan of Pennsylvania, a Jackson supporter and future U.S. president, allegedly suggested to Jackson that he promise to appoint Clay secretary of state in return for his support. Jackson angrily nixed the idea.

Rumors also circulated about a Crawford-Jackson bargain. The idea seemed improbable, given the long-standing animosity between the two that had led Jackson to say, in December 1821, that "I would support the Devil first."[24] But a sighting of their wives together ignited conjecture that Jackson and Crawford were in cahoots.

Speculation about Adams and Clay seemed better justified. On January 8, 1825, Clay wrote a friend that he supported Adams, albeit "with great regret."[25] However, he would not tell anyone how to vote and would certainly seek no personal benefit in exchange for his support; his friends in the House should "throw me out of their consideration" and "be guided solely by the public good."[26] The next day, Clay met with Adams, who described their encounter as follows:

> Mr. Clay came at six, and spent the evening with me in long conversation explanatory of the past and prospective of the future. He said that the time was drawing near when the choice must be made in the House of Representatives of a President . . . [and] that he had been much urged and solicited with regard to the part in the transaction that he should take. . . . The time has now come at which he might be explicit in his communication with me. . . . In the question to come before the House between General Jackson, Mr. Crawford, and myself, he had no hesitation in saying that his preference would be for me.[27]

Adams suggested that Clay had in fact done some bargaining, but not of the improper sort: "He wished me, as far as I might think proper, to satisfy him with regard to some principles of great public importance, but without any personal considerations for himself."[28]

From the beginning, there was widespread suspicion

to the contrary. When a majority of the Ohio and Kentucky delegations (states Clay had carried in November) announced their support for Adams on January 24, an anonymous member of Congress charged that Adams bought Clay's support with the promise to make him secretary of state. Clay demanded that his unnamed colleague come forward. Pennsylvania congressman George Kremner did so, and promised to prove his claim. But when a committee was appointed to investigate the charges, Kremner refused to appear before it.

In a letter to his friend Francis T. Brooke on January 27, Clay reiterated both his bottom-line position and the basis for it: "I have interrogated my conscience as to what I ought to do, and that faithful guide tells me that I ought to vote for Mr. Adams." Far from acknowledging any benefit to himself, Clay cast himself as a martyr. He would catch hell for his choice, but "what is a public man worth if he will not expose himself, on fit occasions, for the good of his country?"[29] According to Adams's diary, Clay visited Adams on January 29 and "sat with me for a couple of hours, discussing all the prospects and probabilities of the Presidential election."[30] Adams offered no elaboration, but that same day, Clay reiterated his choice of Adams in a letter to Francis Preston Blair. His assessment of Adams might qualify as damning with faint praise if there were even a whiff of praise: "I should never have selected [him] if at liberty to draw from the whole mass of our citizens for a President. But there is no danger in his elevation."[31]

In Adams's diary entry for the next day, he observed that "the intriguing for votes is excessive, and the means adopted to obtain them desperate."[32] The nation's capital, if not the nation itself, was understandably obsessed with what Adams circumspectly referred to as "the topic which absorbs all others."[33] He observed that "the flood of visitors is unceasing" and "the excitement of electioneering is kindling into fury."[34] Fury was the right word. Adams claimed to have received an anonymous letter "threatening organized opposition and civil war if Jackson is not chosen."[35]

While Adams always denied that Clay asked for personal benefit in exchange for his support, he did acknowledge such efforts by others on Clay's behalf. In a diary entry on December 17, 1824, he noted the claim by Clay's friend and confidant, Kentucky congressman Robert Letcher, that "Clay would willingly support me if he could thereby serve himself, and the substance of his *meaning* was, that if Clay's friends could *know* that he would have a prominent share in the Administration, that might induce them to vote for me."[36] Adams claimed to give no such assurance, despite ongoing entreaties.

On the morning of January 21, 1825, for example, one congressman "spoke of himself as being entirely devoted to Mr. Clay, and of his hope that [Clay] would be a member of the next Administration," according to Adams's diary. Adams cagily replied that "he would not expect me to enter upon details with regard to the formation of an Administration, but that if I should be elected by the suffrages of the West I should naturally look to the West for much of the support that I should need."[37]

Clay likewise continually disavowed any hanky-panky between himself and Adams. In a typical letter, this one, dated February 4 and addressed to his friend Francis T. Brooke, Clay wrote that "if Mr. Adams is elected, I know not who will be in his cabinet; I know not whether I shall be offered a place in it or not."[38] Their finesse in addressing the situation did nothing to quell concern that a deal between Adams and Clay would determine the election. In his diary entry for February 5, Adams acknowledged the view among some that "if I should be elected, it would only be by Clay's corrupt coalition with me."[39]

On February 9, the House finally voted, and needed only one ballot. Thirteen states voted for Adams, seven for Jackson, and four for Crawford, making Adams the nation's sixth president. All four of the states Clay had won in the Electoral College (Kentucky, Ohio, New York, and Missouri) went for Adams. In New York, Adams allegedly benefited from divine intervention as well as Clay's. With the delegation split, the deciding ballot was cast by the wealthy philanthropist Stephen Van Rensselaer, generally considered a Crawford supporter. Van Rensselaer claimed that, as he was about to cast his ballot, he bent over in prayer. On the floor he spotted a ballot for Adams, and took that as a sign from above.

The next day, Adams expressed his intention to appoint Clay his secretary of state. The charge of a "corrupt bargain" between the two surfaced immediately, dogged both men for the rest of their careers, and contributed to Adams's defeat at Jackson's hands in their rematch four years later. (In 1826, Clay fought a duel over such charges by John Randolph, a senator from Virginia. Though shots were fired, none struck.) Jackson himself unambiguously attributed his defeat in 1824 to an unsavory deal: "The Judas of the West has closed the contract and will receive the thirty pieces of silver. . . . Was there ever witnessed such a bare faced corruption in any country before?"[40]

Was the charge fair? Perhaps not. Adams's diary showed Clay to be among the few men he esteemed. Long before the election reached the House, he observed that Clay's "talents were eminent; his claims from public service considerable."[41] Curiously, as far back as November 30, 1822, two years before the election, Adams made reference to rumors of a deal with Clay whereby the latter would end up secretary of state. Adams dismissed the notion: "There was no understanding or concert between Mr. Clay and me on the subject, and never had been."[42] That would be a claim Adams would repeat many times before and after the House vote in February 1825.

His exhaustive diary, however, says nothing about Clay's role in his victory and precious little about Clay's selection as secretary of state. In his entry for February 9, 1825, Adams recorded his victory in the House in uncharacteristically gushing fashion: "May the blessing of God rest upon the event of this day!"[43] Although he described the results as "completed, very unexpectedly, by a single ballot,"[44] he made no reference to the fact that Clay's allies in the House tipped the balance his way. In his entry for the next day, he mentions a visit by the secretary of the navy, Samuel Southard, and casually relates that "I told him I should offer the Department of State to Mr. Clay."[45]

There had been no prior discussion in the diary as to when or why he settled on Clay, their previous falling out, whether he had considered anyone else, or much of anything related to this choice for a crucial post. The absence of such rumination is especially noteworthy because Adams knew that the appointment of Clay would be contentious. His diary entry for February 11 does note concerns that "if Mr. Clay should be appointed Secretary of State, a determined opposition to the Administration would be organized from the outset."[46] Adams writes, "I am at least forewarned,"[47] but expresses no pause about picking Clay nor explanation for the absence of such pause. Later, in that same entry, he reports telling President Monroe that he would pick Clay "due to his talents and services to the Western section of the Union."[48] That is the full extent of Adams's explanation for the most significant pick of his administration, one that arguably doomed it.

On February 12, he officially offered Clay the secretary of state position, and the latter (according to Adams) "said he would take it into consideration, and answer me as soon as he should have time to consult his friends."[49] Clay's alleged reticence could suggest the absence of a deal between the two, or else Adams choosing to cover their tracks. In his diary entry for February 27, Adams noted "stores of opinion against the appointment of Clay as secretary of state."[50] Before accepting Adams's offer, Clay acknowledged to others the sensitivity of the situation. In a letter to Francis T. Brooke, Clay noted that friends warned him that his becoming secretary of state "would be treated as conclusive evidence of the imputations which have been made against me."[51] That no more stopped him from accepting the offer than it stopped Adams from making it.

It was nearly suicidal for Adams to appoint Clay, and absent an agreement between them, there was no compelling reason for him to do so. In large part for that reason, most historians have concluded that Clay indeed swayed the House to make Adams president in exchange for his appointment as secretary of state—the traditional stepping stone to the presidency, an office Clay would never stop coveting. Ironically, becoming secretary of state may have doomed Clay's larger aspirations. Even during his final bid for the presidency in 1844, Clay's so-called "corrupt bargain" with Adams continually surfaced.

Clay always explained his decision to back Adams as stemming from Jackson's lack of even minimal qualifications for the office. For example, in his letter to Francis Preston Blair dated January 29, 1825, Clay asserted the folly of selecting as president "a Military chieftain, merely because he has won a great victory. . . . I cannot believe that killing 2,500 Englishmen at N. Orleans qualifies for the various, difficult and complicated duties of the Chief

Magistracy."[52] In fact, Clay considered Jackson's military exploits *disqualifying*. Noting that the chief characteristic of the statesman is "a devotion to civil liberty," Clay wrote another friend that "I, therefore, say to you unequivocally, that I can not, consistently with my own principles, support a military man."[53]

The election of 1824 could be seen as a constitutional success story. Notwithstanding the electoral stalemate produced on Election Day, and the passions of the day, the process played out quickly and bloodlessly, producing a president in keeping with established procedures. However, there are several reasons to regard that process as severely flawed.

First, we ended up with a president who lacked popular support. Less than one-third of the voters nationwide chose Adams. Of course, the Electoral College creates an inherent risk of a candidate winning despite receiving fewer votes than another candidate. Rather than pick our president through a single election, we aggregate the results of winner-take-all elections in each state (with the exception of Maine and Nebraska, which award one electoral vote to the winner of the state's congressional districts, as well as two to the statewide winner). Under this system, one can win the presidency despite receiving fewer votes than one's opponent simply by winning a few large states with many electoral votes while losing other states by greater margins. Or, as in 1824, a candidate who receives the greatest number of popular votes *and* electoral votes may fail to win a majority of the latter, sending the election to the House.

On five occasions in U.S. history—1824, 1876, 1888, 2000, and 2016—the candidate who received the most votes was not elected The most extreme case was 1824. Samuel Tilden lost the nationwide popular vote by 3 percent in 1876; Benjamin Harrison by 1 percent in 1888; George W. Bush by half a percentage point in 2000; and Donald Trump by 2 percent in 2016. By contrast, Adams received 38,000 votes fewer than Jackson out of 360,000 cast, a 10 percent gap. In modern parlance, he lost by a landslide. Moreover, unlike the winners in those other four elections, Adams received fewer electoral votes *and* popular votes than his opponent. His elevation to the presidency seems anti-democratic by almost any definition.[54]

Second, although things did play out reasonably swiftly and free of violence, the chance for chaos and popular upheaval loomed. Jackson supporters did not make good on their threat to revolt, but the very fact that such threats were made is sobering.

Third, the election in 1824 was decided by what many regarded as a "corrupt bargain." The widespread suspicion undercut confidence in U.S. democracy. In the run-up to the House vote, Adams himself expressed concern that, if it were perceived that he prevailed because of a deal with Clay, "the people would be so disgusted with this that there would be a systematic and determined opposition from the beginning, so that the

Administration could not get along."[55] He proved prophetic. Adams received little cooperation from Jackson supporters in Congress and, in 1828, lost his rematch to Jackson decisively.

Assuming that Adams and Clay did strike a deal, was it in fact corrupt? On the one hand, for a politician to support a candidate for office in expectation (or even an explicit promise) of a position in his administration could be seen as time-honored horse trading. However, the notion that someone achieves the presidency because another candidate offers his support to the highest bidder seems obviously problematic. In the case of 1824, the easiest resolution of this dilemma is to emphasize the covert nature of the deal (if there was one) between Adams and Clay. Even if it was fine for the two to strike a bargain, the American people deserved to know about it. Ditto the Senate that had to determine whether to confirm Clay as secretary of state.

A full consideration of the propriety of the alleged actions of Clay and Adams is beyond the scope of this book. What matters for our purposes is the judgment rendered by the American people, and the fact that the arrangement the people judged harshly came about in large part because of the way we elect a president.

Conversely, Adams's loss to Jackson in 1828 could be seen as a cleansing election, an antidote to the toxic backroom dealing that put Adams in office in the first place. So too, the corrupt bargain would have been partially thwarted had the Senate chosen not to confirm

Clay as secretary of state. Thus, one could look at the election of 1824 and give the Constitution one or two cheers. While it failed to prevent the crisis, it contained corrective mechanisms that could and to some extent did limit the damage. But should we settle for a system that predictably produces crises?

THREE

THE ELECTION OF 1876

In America in 1876, national pride intersected with national insecurity. The year marked the 100th anniversary of U.S. Independence, an event greeted with mass celebration, including the ballyhooed Centennial Exposition in Philadelphia, a grand display of the nation's achievements. At the same time, the Civil War, little more than a decade old, remained a vivid reminder of the nation's flaws and fragility. Moreover, if the centennial served to unite the nation, the ongoing fight over Reconstruction reinforced the nation's still bitter divisions.

Against that backdrop, Democrats sought to win their first presidential election in forty years, while the Republicans aimed to extend their four consecutive terms in the White House. (There were four Whig Party presidents during the 1840s and '50s.) The fight for the nomination of both parties was wide open. Unlike the three previous cycles, in which Republicans more or less anointed the incumbent presidents, Lincoln and Grant, they had no prohibitive favorite (given Grant's intent to step down after two terms, following the precedent established by George Washington and adhered to by every president since). The Democrats, too, lacked a clear front-runner.

The Republican field included three prominent U.S. senators: Maine's James Blaine, New York's Roscoe Conkling, and Indiana's Oliver Morton. Morton, who as governor of Indiana during the Civil War had supplied the Union far more troops than requested, suffered a stroke in 1865 that left him permanently disabled but did not diminish his lust for the presidency. Blaine and Conkling, who sowed the seeds of their candidacies for years, were such bitter enemies that Conkling, asked whether he could imagine supporting Blaine, replied, "I don't engage in criminal practice."[56] Another Republican candidate, Grant's secretary of the treasury Benjamin Bristow, was a hero of the liberal wing of the party who advocated less aggressive policies toward the South.

Blaine, who had been Speaker of the House for six years before his recent selection to the Senate, was widely perceived as the front-runner. At the opposite end of the spectrum was dark horse Rutherford B. Hayes. A successful criminal defense attorney (with a degree from Harvard Law School) who had represented a number of escaped slaves and a Union general badly wounded in battle, Hayes was elected to Congress in 1864 and re-elected in 1866, but resigned shortly thereafter to seek the governorship of Ohio. He was elected to that position in 1868, and served two terms before retiring in 1872. However, three years later the Republicans drafted him to run again for governor. No sooner was Hayes again elected to that position than his name began to be bandied about as a long-shot presidential candidate.

In the run-up to the Republican Convention in June in Cincinnati, all of the candidates craved the endorsement of President Grant, and courted him assiduously. The other major activity in the spring of 1876 was the holding of state conventions to select delegates committed to one of the candidates. However, many states opted to eschew the declared candidates and instead support a "favorite son" (their own governor or some other local politician) in order to maintain their flexibility and leverage at the national convention.

Blaine might have been a more commanding favorite if he hadn't been dogged by charges of corruption, especially the claim that shortly after he was elected to Congress in 1863, he received a $64,000 bribe from Union Pacific Railroad. It wasn't until 1880, when Blaine again sought his party's nomination, that Democrats trotted out their famous rallying cry: "James, James, James G. Blaine, the continental liar from the state of Maine." But questions about Blaine's probity surfaced throughout the run-up to the 1876 Republican Convention in Cincinnati. A lengthy congressional investigation into his alleged misdeeds was ongoing when, on June 11, while walking to church on a hot day, Blaine collapsed and fell to the ground unconscious. The *New York Sun*, a Democratic-run newspaper, ran an article titled "Blaine Feigns a Faint."[57] That others shared skepticism about Blaine's alleged faint indicates the widespread doubts about his character, not to mention the fact that "fake news" long preceded the forty-fifth presidency.

The fainting incident was a double-edged sword for Blaine: It postponed the congressional investigation into his affairs, but it concerned delegates to the Republican Convention, who were already assembling in Cincinnati. (Blaine recovered just before the convention convened.) Even so, he entered the convention sufficiently confident to send out feelers to Hayes about the latter's interest in the vice presidency. Hayes nixed the idea, writing a friend that "I have the greatest aversion to being a candidate on the ticket with a man whose record as an upright public man is to be in question."[58]

The convention opened on June 14, with a few days devoted to speeches, back-room meetings and maneuvering, and debate over the party platform. The latter served as a reminder that, over a decade after Lee surrendered at Appomattox, the Civil War had not really ended. The Republican platform that emerged in Cincinnati called for "permanent pacification of the Southern section of the Union" and accused the Democratic Party of "being the same in character and spirit as when it sympathized with treason."

The nominating process commenced on Friday, June 16. As was typical in the pre-modern era, the outcome was unknowable because no delegates were bound by primaries (there were none) or anything else. Blaine, still the perceived front-runner, faced an anybody-but-Blaine coalition that could thwart him if it coalesced around any of the other six names placed in nomination.

On the first ballot, Blaine received the most votes, 285, but still ninety-four short of the 379 needed for the nomination. Morton was a distant second with 124, Bristow third with 113, followed by Conkling's ninety-nine. Rutherford B. Hayes received only sixty-one votes, just seventeen from outside his home state of Ohio, making him closer to a favorite son than a serious contender. The clerk immediately called for a second ballot, but the results hardly changed—Blaine gained eleven votes, no one else more than five. Two more ballots barely moved the needle. Before the fifth ballot, the leader of the Michigan delegation, who opposed Blaine, pushed his delegation to vote Hayes as a compromise choice, and other states followed suit. Hayes gained thirty-six votes on the fifth ballot, while Blaine lost six. But the movement was not linear. On the sixth ballot, all of North Carolina's eleven delegates who had switched from Blaine to Hayes now switched back to Blaine. Overall, Blaine gained twenty-two votes, reaching 308, whereas Hayes, despite the North Carolina defection, picked up nine more.

It had become a two-man race between the favorite and the dark horse, the former with the most passionate support and opposition alike and the latter exciting little passion in either direction. Finally, on the seventh ballot, Hayes received 384 votes, five more than needed for the nomination, and Blaine 351. The Republican nomination for president belonged to Governor Rutherford B. Hayes.

The process reflected, first and foremost, dislike of Blaine and the need to find *someone*. The great nineteenth-century historian Henry Adams offered this contemporary assessment of Hayes: He was "a third rate nonentity whose only recommendation is that he is obnoxious to no one."[59] In those days, the convention, not the presidential nominee, selected his running mate. The delegates opted for an inoffensive and obscure New York congressman, William Wheeler, primarily because he was popular among his colleagues and offered geographical balance to the ticket. (When Hayes heard, he wrote to his wife Lucy: "I am ashamed to say: Who *is Wheeler?*")[60] Blaine, for his part, took the defeat well, graciously congratulating Hayes and pledging his full support in the general election.

Hayes's opponent in that race, Samuel Tilden, secured the Democratic nomination with far less intra-party division and drama, and figured to pose a real threat to Hayes in the general election. The Democrats had suffered terrible defeats during and in the aftermath of the Civil War, but a Wall Street panic in 1873 leveled the political playing field. In 1874, a so-called "Tidal Wave" gave Democrats a majority in the House and, it was believed, a realistic shot at the White House.

Tilden, like Hayes a successful lawyer (with an undergraduate degree from Yale and law degree from NYU), was an aloof figure who made his name as the prosecutor who broke up the notorious Tweed Ring that dominated New York City politics for a decade. He rode a wave of positive publicity to election as a state assemblyman, where he was ahead of his time as a machine politician, gathering an extraordinary amount of information about citizens' voting records and distributing targeted campaign literature accordingly. Tilden was elected governor of New York in 1874, defeating the popular incumbent, John Dix, during the Democratic Tidal Wave. He used his platform as governor of the nation's most populous state to criticize alleged corruption in the Grant administration, and the resulting attention elevated him to the status of presidential contender.

The Democratic field eventually included Delaware senator Thomas Bayard (whose grandfather played a pivotal role in breaking the Jefferson-Burr deadlock in 1800), Indiana Governor Thomas Hendricks, former Ohio governor William Allen (defeated by Hayes in 1875), General Winfield Hancock, and a few also-rans. The party convention took place in St. Louis in late June. The Tilden campaign touted the candidate's electability in a general election, emphasizing that New York would be a large, crucial swing state. This was back in the day when, to a large extent, party bosses controlled their state's delegates, and the Tilden camp was comfortable moving and schmoozing in smoke-filled rooms.

On June 27, the convention's first day, the Democratic National Committee selected a Tilden supporter as convention president. The next day was given over to approving a platform largely drafted by Tilden's people. The balloting began on June 29, and on the first ballot

Tilden picked up 401.5 votes, easily outpacing the runner-up, Hendricks, who tallied 140.5, but falling well short of the 491 needed for the nomination. Between the first and second ballots, Tilden's adroit operatives convinced several delegations that their man was the inevitable nominee and that they should cast their lot with him sooner rather than later. On the second ballot, he received 535 votes and the nomination. Hendricks was the virtually unanimous choice for vice president. The Democrats were united by a fervent desire to regain the White House after a long exile, and chose the ticket that seemed best designed for that purpose.

From the beginning, a close contest between Hayes and Tilden was expected. In the wake of several scandals plaguing the outgoing Grant administration, the issue of civil service reform favored Tilden and the Democrats. The Republican platform echoed the Democrats' call for such reform, but as the candidate of the incumbent party, Hayes needed to do more. With that in mind, he pledged to serve only one term if elected.

Another prominent issue was Reconstruction and the future of African Americans. Republicans were the more progressive party on this issue and labeled Democrats the "rebellion party." Tilden himself, however, had opposed slavery and supported the Union during the Civil War. In part for that reason, Hayes, though a staunch abolitionist long before the Civil War, declined to emphasize racial justice issues. The Republican standard bearer had supported the Thirteenth, Fourteenth, and Fifteenth Amendments to the Constitution that enshrined formal political equality for African Americans, but he did not believe the races equal and gave only lukewarm support to Reconstruction policies designed to force further concessions from the South with respect to the treatment of blacks.

In keeping with the American tradition, the general election campaign featured little actual campaigning by the candidates themselves. This suited Hayes and Tilden, who had their hands full governing their respective states. (In addition, Tilden was still recovering from a mild stroke he suffered in February.) Perhaps because there were few substantive differences between the candidates, their personal peccadilloes took center stage. Tilden stood accused of filing a false income tax return in 1863, courtesy of a *New York Times* report that followed months of digging into the financial records of their home state governor. The issue was neutralized when it turned out that Hayes had paid zero federal income tax in 1868 and '69.

Though there were no public opinion polls in 1876, that doesn't mean the nation awoke on Election Day without a clue as to who would win. There are always tea leaves to read, and in November 1876, most people who read them concluded that Samuel Tilden would be the next president of the United States. On November 7, 1876, 8.5 million Americans cast their ballot for president, a full 2 million more than voted in 1872. We remember the "Dewey Beats Truman" *Chicago Tribune* headline in 1948, because Truman famously held it aloft to be photographed. It is less well known that, on November 8, 1876, another Chicago newspaper got ahead of itself. The *Chicago Daily News* reported that Tilden won the presidency "by a very considerable majority of the electoral vote."[61] It was not alone. In its headline, the *New York Sun* flatly declared "Tilden is Elected," and newspapers around the country followed suit.[62]

The reality was that Tilden received 250,000 more votes than Hayes and enjoyed an Electoral College lead of nineteen (184 to 165), but three states—South Carolina, Florida, and Louisiana—remained too close to call. That left Tilden one vote short of an Electoral College majority. If Hayes captured the three cliff-hanger states, he would have the requisite 185 electoral votes to become president. And all three of these states, undergoing Reconstruction, were controlled by Republicans.

This was the first crisis-ridden presidential election since 1824, and Democrats hoped it would follow suit in one crucial respect. The earlier election ended up being resolved by the House of Representatives. Tilden welcomed that possibility, because Democrats controlled the House; he would be elected if things took that turn. Accordingly, while Democrats hoped that Tilden would win an outright majority of the electoral vote, their Plan B was to disqualify enough electors so that neither candidate amassed a majority. This may seem odd today, but in the nineteenth century, substantial mischief surrounded the Electoral College. In 1856, for example, on account of a blizzard, Wisconsin's electors met the day after the congressionally prescribed date. Their votes were accepted, but only after two days of acrimonious debate in Congress. In 1872, Congress refused to count Arkansas's electoral votes ostensibly because the certificate of return lacked the particular seal required by federal law.

While the participants in the 1876 drama looked to past elections for guidance, they had no way of knowing that their election would be oddly echoed more than a century later. Historians who study the 1876 election remark on the "eerie similarities to the 2000 dispute over Florida."[63] To take just one example, shortly after Election Day in 1876, dozens of politicians and lawyers from each party descended on Florida (and the other disputed states)—to observe, protest, and litigate. To take another, one party (in this case, the Democrats) was widely accused of suppressing the African American vote in Florida and elsewhere.

One difference between the two elections is that the atmosphere after Election Day in 2000, tense though it may have seemed, was far calmer. The post-vote maneuvering in 1876 produced sufficient chaos and acrimony to prompt rumblings of a second Civil War. With the first barely a decade behind the young nation, animosities remained high. Tilden supporters in particular threatened to raise vigilante armies if their man was denied the White House ("Tilden or blood" was their rallying cry), and President Ulysses S. Grant dispatched troops to the three disputed states to keep the peace. Some Democrats called for Grant's impeachment, but people in Florida,

Louisiana, and South Carolina welcomed the protection. The military presence prevented violence, but not chicanery. As political scientist Norman Ornstein succinctly explains, both before and after Election Day, "There was bribery, forgery, and ballot-box stuffing by both sides."[64]

That is not to suggest symmetrical behavior by the two candidates during the post–Election Day dispute. While Hayes lobbied politicians for support, Tilden devoted the next several weeks to writing a book-length study about the history of presidential elections. He planned to give a copy to every member of Congress, believing that the history supported his position in the Electoral College and, more naively, that congressmen could be swayed by the merits of the case.

In Florida, Tilden won the initial count by a mere ninety-four votes. However, calls came to invalidate the votes in a number of precincts because of alleged improprieties. The state's three-person canvassing board consisted of two Republicans and one Democrat. Most of their determinations with respect to challenged votes broke down along party lines, with the board rejecting votes for Tilden and upholding votes for Hayes. One of the Republican canvassers, Florida's secretary of state Samuel McLin, admitted in testimony before Congress two years later that he approached the work "as a very active partisan. . . . I shall always lean to my own party, and give my decision in its favor, even at the hazard of straining a point."[65]

Such straining included discounting Tilden votes

based on technicalities. The board invalidated two precincts that together gave Tilden a net gain of 354 votes because the election inspectors left the ballots unattended during a dinner break. They rejected the ballots from another precinct, which produced a 342-vote Tilden margin because the election inspectors did not count the ballots until the day after the election and outside of public view. Perhaps these rulings were defensible, but not in conjunction with other decisions declining to reject the tally in precincts won by Hayes despite evidence of overt fraud.[66] As a result of the board's handiwork, Hayes won the state by 924 votes. Most historians to study the matter maintain that, had the board acted impartially, Tilden would have won Florida. (To be sure, most of them believe that Hayes would have won the state handily but for intimidation and other means of suppressing African Americans from voting.) Some fair-minded observers at the time reached the same conclusion. President Grant sent Francis Barlow, a former Civil War hero, to Florida to observe the count. Though himself a Republican, Barlow claimed that Tilden won the state and that the decision favoring Hayes resulted from pure partisanship.

On December 5, one day before the electors met to cast their ballots, the canvassing board completed its work and certified Hayes the winner of the state. The next day, while the Republican electors cast their ballots for Hayes and sent these votes to Congress (certified by Florida's Republican governor), Democrats did the same! The Democratic votes were certified by the state's attorney general, who happened to be the one Democrat on the canvassing board. Accordingly, Congress received a pair of certified slates of twenty-five electoral votes, one for each candidate.

Democrats filed suit in state court, and a Democratic judge ruled that Tilden's slate of electors, not Hayes's, was valid under state law. Meanwhile, on Election Day, Florida voters had replaced the majority Republican legislature with a majority of Democrats. (On account of a court ruling following a disputed election, a Democrat won the governor's race as well.) On January 17, the newly sworn-in Democratic legislature reconstituted the canvassing board to include all three Democrats, and ordered the board to re-canvas the presidential ballots. To no one's surprise, the new board found that Tilden won the state. The new Democratic governor certified this finding, and sent Congress a third certification—so that two Florida certifications now favored Tilden.

The situation was similar in Louisiana and South Carolina, both of which experienced blatant fraud. While many blacks in these states were prevented from voting, many whites voted more than once. In South Carolina, which lacked voter registration laws, the number of votes exceeded the number of potential voters. Apparently some people took seriously the admonition to vote early and often. So too, many Georgians allegedly crossed the Savannah River to cast votes in South Carolina before returning home to cast a lawful vote. In one precinct in Louisiana with a total of 3,000 registered voters, roughly two-thirds of whom were black, the tally showed Tilden receiving 1,743 votes and Hayes . . . zero. Throughout these states, the two parties hurled credible accusations and counter-accusations of fraud. In South Carolina, they moved beyond accusation: Members of the canvassing board briefly found themselves in prison, before a panel of federal judges granted writs of habeas corpus to free them.

South Carolina and Louisiana, like Florida, sent to Congress competing certificates of electoral votes, albeit only two rather than three. In each state, the canvassing board, controlled by Republicans, determined that Hayes had won, and the Republican governor certified the electoral votes in Hayes's favor. In Louisiana, the votes for Tilden were certified by Democrat John McEnery, who *claimed* to be the rightful governor. (In 1872, McEnery lost a disputed election for governor.) In South Carolina the Democratic electors essentially certified themselves, sending their votes to Washington with no official signature of certification.

Simply as a matter of math, the situation in Louisiana seemed most egregious to Democrats. Tilden won the original vote there by 6,000, much larger than the margin by which he seemed to win Florida and South Carolina, but canvassing boards invalidated roughly 13,000 Democratic votes due to alleged "intimidation." Many African Americans, who overwhelmingly favored Republicans, were undeniably intimidated. The exact basis for discounting particular ballots was less clear.

In Louisiana, Democrats questioned the legitimacy

of the canvassing board for good reason, since state law prohibited the formation of a canvassing board whose members all belonged to the same party. When the lone Democrat on the board resigned in 1874, the Republicans refused to fill the vacancy. Accordingly, the board that ruled for Hayes consisted of four Republicans and zero Democrats. In an effort to win the public's confidence, the board did hold twelve public sessions. It did not help, however, that the board was presided over by James Madison Wells, a notoriously sleazy politician considered open to bribes.[67] It may or may not be coincidental that, after the Louisiana board helped him become president, Hayes appointed Wells and two other board members to federal positions.

While the main event took place in Florida, Louisiana, and South Carolina, Democrats also raised an issue concerning one of the three electoral votes in Oregon, a state that indisputably went for Hayes. The U.S. Constitution forbids presidential electors from "holding an office of Trust or Profit under the United States," and one Hayes elector was a local postmaster. However, under Oregon law, an ineligible elector can be replaced prior to December 6. Accordingly, when the objection to this elector surfaced shortly after the November 7 election, he resigned his position as postmaster and was reappointed to his position as an elector by the other electors. Oregon's Democratic governor nevertheless replaced him with a Tilden elector. The governor then certified two electoral votes for Hayes but the third for Tilden, whereas the secretary of state certified three electoral votes for Hayes. Thus, as with the other three disputed states, Congress received dueling certifications.

The Democrats did not expect to prevail in Oregon; they were trying to force Congress to scrutinize rather than automatically accept the states' certifications of electors. If Congress did that with respect to Oregon (and if it didn't, Tilden had his 185th elector), it would have to do so as well for Louisiana, Florida, and South Carolina. But, as Supreme Court Justice William Rehnquist observed in his book about the 1876 election, the Democrats' ploy hurt them in the court of public opinion because "the Democratic position in Oregon . . . was even more egregious than the Republican position in Florida and Louisiana."[68]

The situation involving competing certifications of electors is not directly addressed by the Constitution. Indeed, when it comes to the Electoral College, the Constitution says little and leaves many potentially troubling situations unaddressed. The previous presidential election, in 1872, provided a bizarre illustration. The Democratic candidate, Horace Greeley, died three weeks after the election, prior to the date on which members of the Electoral College met. Greeley had earned eighty electoral votes, but could electors cast valid ballots for a dead man? The Constitution doesn't say. Some electors did so, but the joint House-Senate committee tasked with receiving and recording the votes chose not to count votes for Greeley.

The Twelfth Amendment to the Constitution provides that each state's electors must send their certificates to the president of the U.S. Senate, who "shall, in the presence of the Senate and the House of Representatives, open all the certificates and the votes shall then be counted." With respect to the disputed states in the Hayes-Tilden race, Republicans interpreted this language to give the president of the Senate the authority to choose from among the competing certifications. The Constitution makes the vice president the president of the Senate, but President Grant's vice president, Henry Wilson, had died a year earlier and had not been replaced. (Prior to ratification of the Twenty-Fifth Amendment in 1967, vice presidential vacancies went unfilled.) The acting president of the Senate (or "president pro tempore"), Senator Thomas Ferry, was a Republican, which explains the Republicans' interpretation of the Twelfth Amendment. Democrats pointed to a different constitutional provision, the one giving the House authority to choose the president if no candidate receives a majority of electoral votes, and argued that the House therefore controls the count and should determine which slates of electors to accept. Democrats controlled the House, which explains their interpretation of the Twelfth Amendment.

In early December, the House and Senate each appointed special committees to investigate and resolve the situation in the four disputed states. Each committee held extensive hearings, but they needn't have bothered. The Republican-controlled Senate committee found that

Hayes had won each of the states; the Democrat-controlled House committee determined Tilden to be the winner. In each case, the committee's determination broke down perfectly along party lines.

This impasse raised the very real possibility of two presidents enjoying simultaneous swearings-in on March 4. It might make for a great political novel, with the plot eventually involving the military facing orders from two putative commanders-in-chief. But precisely because the two branches were controlled by different parties, no easy solution suggested itself. Moderates in the two parties undertook a predictable bipartisan approach: formation of a joint congressional committee. The committee included seven House members and seven senators; seven Democrats and seven Republicans. During the next two weeks, every proposal on how to proceed produced a seven-seven deadlock. Finally, someone proposed and everyone embraced a way to break the stalemate: creating a fifteen-member commission consisting of five senators, five House members, and five Supreme Court justices. The commission's determinations would be binding unless rejected by both houses of Congress.

Choosing an odd number of members of the commission made good sense in one way but not another. It prevented a tie vote but raised the obvious question of which party would have the extra member. That, in turn, depended on another vexing question: Which five Supreme Court justices would serve? It was originally proposed that the justices be picked by lot, prompting Tilden to object that "I might lose the presidency, but I will not raffle for it."[69] Members of Congress next proposed designating the five most senior justices, which fortuitously included two Democrats, two Republicans, and David Davis, a self-described independent who had not voted in the presidential election. Davis was an enormous man (allegedly 300 pounds) who played an enormous role in the 1876 election by playing no role at all.

The Illinoisan was a close friend of Abraham Lincoln, his campaign manager in 1860, and appointed by Lincoln to the Supreme Court in 1862. He was a Whig-turned-Republican who became disillusioned by the Republican Party to the point that, when his appointment on the election commission of 1876 was proposed, Republicans balked, claiming that Davis was "to all intents and purposes, a Democrat," and thus would tip the commission in Tilden's favor.[70]

The joint committee, which was created by a bill signed into law by President Grant on January 29, solved the problem by naming four justices, two Democrats and two Republicans, and tasking these four with selecting the fifth. It was fully expected that they would choose Davis, and that his selection by a bipartisan group of his colleagues would enhance public confidence. But the plan quickly went awry: Prior to the selection of Davis, the Democratic-controlled Illinois legislature selected him as a United States senator. Republicans cried foul, alleging that the Democrats were essentially bribing Davis, the quid pro quo being his vote for Tilden when the electoral commission made its decision.[71] If that was indeed the plan, it was too clever by half: Davis declared that, as a soon-to-be-sworn-in senator, he could not in good conscience serve on the commission. He received dozens of telegrams and some in-person appeals urging him to reconsider, but he proved steadfast. Some historians speculate that Davis, who long eyed the presidency himself (and for a while had been considered a viable candidate in 1872), saw little value in serving on a commission whose decision was guaranteed to infuriate half the country.

When the four justices huddled to select a fifth, by a three-one vote they nevertheless tapped Davis, thinking he might be persuaded yet. However, Davis declined their offer. The justices then unanimously selected Joseph Bradley, a moderate Republican regarded as the least partisan of the remaining justices. Representative Abram Hewitt of New York, chairman of the Democratic National Committee and Tilden's campaign manager, considered Bradley "a man of the highest integrity."[72] Not all Democrats concurred. The Democrat-leaning *New York Sun* editorialized that Bradley was "a partisan to whom his party never looked in vain."[73] The *Chicago Tribune* split the difference, reporting that no one knew what to expect from Bradley; Republicans "fear that he is more [impartial] lawyer than Republican, and the Democrats fear that he is more Republican than lawyer."[74]

In a process that stretched out over a month, and included public hearings featuring learned presentations by the nation's most prestigious lawyers for both sides, the commission (which included future president James Garfield, then a member of the House) ruled in Hayes's favor with respect to the disputes in all four states—by an 8-7 party-line vote. In each case, the principal issue was whether the commission, on behalf of Congress, had the authority to "look behind" the canvassing board's determination. This difficult question divided legal scholars at the time and ever since. Unfortunately, when it came to the commission's findings, as well as Congress's decision whether to approve or reject them, perspective on legal issues seemed determined by political allegiance. The Democrat-controlled House voted to reject the commission's findings, whereas the Republican-controlled Senate endorsed them. Since the resolution creating the commission stipulated that its findings would be followed unless rejected by both Houses, it appeared to be case closed and Hayes president. But the Democrats refused to acquiesce just yet.

On February 28, the House and Senate met in the constitutionally required joint session to do the final vote tally, at this point seemingly a mere formality. And so it went, with the alphabetical call of the states and recording of their electoral votes, from A through U. That covered all four of the disputed states, whose Republican votes were recorded without incident. But when Vermont was called, Representative Hewitt rose and asked to be recognized. Hewitt explained, "I hold in my hand a package which purports to contain electoral votes from the State of Vermont." He offered it to Senator Ferry (presiding as president pro tempore), who replied that he could not consider new materials at that late date. Ferry had in his possession Vermont's five certified votes for Hayes, and the last thing he wanted was yet another contested state, particularly after the previous four had been resolved. But House Democrats did not accept his ruling. A representative from Illinois screamed and gesticulated wildly until the Senate walked out, convened separately, and accepted Vermont's certification of votes for Hayes.

What was going on? Hewitt and the Democrats had contrived the Vermont dispute in the hopes of reconvening the commission and running out the clock—preventing resolution of the matter until Inauguration Day. They were playing with fire, since dueling inaugurations would have created national chaos, and by this time, on account of the commission's decision, Republicans held the high ground. It was difficult to imagine a winning end game for the Democrats, but many of them, feeling cheated, did not feel compelled to accept reality.

The House met on March 1, three days before the scheduled inauguration, and found Democrats split between those wishing to acquiesce in Hayes's election to spare the nation chaos and others willing to take that risk. In the session of the House that followed, fights nearly erupted (with some members brandishing pistols, presumably for protection from the public), and the speaker had to call in the sergeant at arms to restore order. Hours of debate ensued. A decisive moment came when Louisiana Representative William Levy, a Democrat, passed along crucial intelligence. He and other Southern Democrats had met with close associates of Hayes and, he hinted broadly, received reassurances that a President Hayes would treat white Americans in the South well. In particular, Hayes allegedly agreed to withdraw federal troops that propped up Reconstructionist governors.

Accordingly, Levy urged his fellow Democrats to accept Hayes's election. The tide turned against obstruction. Even so, on March 3 the House passed a resolution declaring that Tilden received 196 electoral votes and "was thereby duly elected President." But by this point the candidate himself had publicly conceded, and congressional Democrats went down without further fight beyond their toothless resolution. Outside the halls of Congress, all wasn't so copacetic. Some Democrats around the nation called for armed rebellion, an idea allegedly entertained by George McClellan, the Civil War general and Democratic presidential candidate in 1864.

As noted, legal scholars disagree about the propriety of the commission's findings in favor of Hayes. The commission received the imprimatur of none other than Justice-then-Senator Davis, apparently considered by many the only person in government capable of an impartial opinion. Davis privately opined that the commission ruled properly, and "no good lawyer, not a strict partisan, could decide otherwise."[75] Few Democrats agreed. Justice Stephen Field, who served on the commission, considered its work "a gigantic conspiracy and fraud."[76] Justice Bradley, in particular, came in for harsh criticism (not to mention death threats), such as the *New York Sun*'s view that he "will be known in history as the infamous eighth man who, without scruple and without shame, cast his vote every time to uphold the frauds."[77] Even Hayes's hometown newspaper, the *Cincinnati Enquirer*, darkly declared that "by the grace of Joe Bradley . . . the monster fraud of the century is consummated."[78] Rumors circulated, supported by shreds of circumstantial evidence, that Bradley had written an opinion favoring Tilden with respect to Florida's electors, and changed his mind only as a result of last-minute pressure from Republican politicians.[79]

It is unclear what would have happened without the assurances reported by Congressman Levy. Perhaps cooler heads would nevertheless have prevailed. Or perhaps the unthinkable—two presidential inaugurations, two would-be presidents, and a grave constitutional crisis. In any event, Hayes aimed for conciliation in his inaugural address, directly addressing his controversial election. He acknowledged that "peculiar circumstances" led to the creation of the commission, and despite the "reputation for integrity and intelligence" of its members, "opinion will vary widely as to the wisdom of several of the conclusions announced by that tribunal." That, he claimed, was inevitable in legal matters, as the losing party will inevitably feel wronged. The new president urged Americans to regard the peaceful resolution as "an occasion for general rejoicing."[80]

Indeed, one might be tempted to conclude that the system worked, or at least that the guardrails held, insofar as the election was resolved without bloodshed. But we should not fool ourselves into thinking that a peaceful resolution was inevitable—even apart from the fact that, in December, a bullet into Hayes's house narrowly missed him. Thirty years later, Pulitzer Prize–winning historian James Ford Rhodes claimed that everyone who lived through the Hayes-Tilden imbroglio, or studied the evidence thereafter, "cannot avoid the conviction that the country was on the verge of civil war."[81] To say the system worked because a second civil war was narrowly averted is to set the bar awfully low. A process that played out primarily in partisan terms can hardly be judged a success.

In his inaugural address, Hayes claimed that the commission's decision was "entitled to the fullest confidence of the American people."[82] That judgment seems naïve or self-serving. Even if one agrees with the commission's decision, it was a serious source of concern that our election system lent itself to the kind of chaos and disenchantment that prevailed for four fraught months and left half the nation feeling cheated.

As it happens, President Rutherford B. Hayes did indeed adopt a conciliatory stance toward white supremacists, effectively ending Reconstruction. That pleased but did not placate Democrats, who routinely referred to the president as "Rutherfraud" and "His Fraudulence." During the post–Election Day drama, President Grant stated that "either party can afford to be disappointed in the result, but the country cannot afford to have the result tainted by the suspicion of illegal or false returns."[83]

Alas, as in 1824, suspicions of skullduggery only grew over time, and a cloud of illegitimacy hovered over the new president. Hayes served one unremarkable term after an election that was anything but.

What lessons were learned from the 1876 election? Not enough, at least to judge by the fact that the nation experienced something fairly close to a repeat, albeit more than a century later. No constitutional amendments were adopted in the wake of the '76 donnybrook, although in 1887 Congress did pass the Electoral Count Act (ECA). The ECA clarifies that Congress should honor only those electoral vote certifications made by the state's executive, unless a majority in both houses of Congress rejects that certification. The ECA also provides procedural guidance for the conduct of the joint House-Senate committee receiving the certified votes, and incentivizes states to send in the certifications in timely fashion by establishing that electoral votes certified six days before the Electoral College meets must be accepted by Congress. The latter provision played a key role in the 2000 election but, as we shall see, did more harm than good.

During the debate over the ECA, Senator John Sherman, a Republican from Ohio, asserted that failure to provide a proper means to resolve disputed presidential elections "is more dangerous to the future of this country than probably any other."[84] He may have been right. However, as shall become apparent in the next chapter, ECA failed to prevent another intra-state fight over a state's electors, much less to address a number of other existing or potential problems with the Electoral College. In the sober assessment of Professor Edward Foley, an election law expert and author of an invaluable study of disputed elections, "the Hayes-Tilden dispute exposed structural frailties in the nation's constitutional order that . . . were unchanged in 1876 and remain unchanged today."[85]

As for what lessons *should* be learned from the 1876 crisis, we will revisit that question after first reacquainting ourselves with the delayed sequel: the election of 2000.

FOUR

THE ELECTION OF 2000

Reflecting on the 2000 presidential election, one might detect the handiwork of a cosmic joker. Consider that the winner was partly determined by elderly Jews who, eager to elect the nation's first Jewish vice president, prevented that result by accidentally voting for someone many regard as anti-Semitic. Palm Beach, Florida's, so-called butterfly ballot, ironically designed by Democrats, led many confused Gore-Lieberman supporters to cast their ballot for Pat Buchanan. Consider, too, that the entire election nationwide came down to a virtual tie, leading to virtual anarchy, in a state that happened to be governed by the brother of one of the candidates.

Before its absurdist last chapter, the 2000 campaign lacked a theme. Like the presidential campaign of 1876, it featured relatively little policy debate. After Bill Clinton's two terms as president, a period marked by economic growth at home and peace abroad, Democrats figured they would win if they played things safe. Clinton's loyal vice president, Al Gore, easily captured the party's nomination over Bill Bradley, the former U.S. senator who advanced a more ambitious policy agenda. As the party's nominee, Gore put forth few meaningful positions, more or less running for Clinton's third term—minus the scandals that attached to the president and culminated in his impeachment.

Given those scandals, Republicans, too, figured they would win if they played things safe. Party leaders pretty much anointed as their nominee George W. Bush, the bland governor of Texas and son of a former president. Though Senator John McCain, the maverick Arizonan, interrupted Bush's coronation by winning a few early primaries, Bush secured the nomination with relative ease. He offered "compassionate conservatism," an opaque formulation suggesting that he didn't plan to stir up trouble or veer terribly far from Clinton's path. Green Party candidate Ralph Nader, who received almost 3 million votes, claimed that abortion was the only issue separating the major parties, quipping that Democrats and Republicans were the pro-choice corporate party and pro-life corporate party respectively.

A lackluster campaign in a complacent and evenly divided nation produced the closest presidential election in U.S. history. On the night of the election, November 7, it became apparent that the winner of the Electoral College would be whichever candidate won Florida. The networks first called the state, and hence the nation, for Gore, then flipped and called it for Bush, but in each case acted prematurely. After the networks projected Bush as the winner at 2:00 a.m. Eastern Standard Time, Gore called his rival and conceded. He retracted the concession hours later when it became apparent that the race was in fact too close to call.

When the votes were finally all in on November 8, Bush enjoyed a minuscule 1,784-vote lead out of nearly 6 million ballots cast—thanks, in part, to the confusing butterfly ballot and perhaps the alleged purge of some African Americans from the voter rolls.[86] (The latter possibility was one of many similarities to the 1876 election.) Post-election, nothing could be done about voter suppression, and while Palm Beach voters filed a suit concerning the butterfly ballot, Gore's legal team recognized its futility and did not join in. Florida's Supreme Court eventually ruled that the flawed ballot design did not violate state law and, in any event, could not be remedied.

Even without considering the votes Gore may have lost to badly designed ballots and voter suppression, as well as the 97,000 Floridians who cast ballots for Nader, most of whom presumably preferred Gore to Bush, the state was ridiculously close. Because Bush's infinitesimal 0.03 percent margin was less than 0.5 percent, Florida law called for a mandatory machine recount. That recount, undertaken on November 9, narrowed Bush's lead to a mere 327 votes. A little-known but potentially decisive fact is that eighteen counties, encompassing roughly a fourth of the statewide vote, apparently never conducted the required machine recount.[87]

Florida law gives each county's canvassing board

discretion to begin a manual recount upon a candidate's or party's request. When a board does so, it must sample 1 percent of the vote. If, based on that sample, it finds sufficient basis for believing that an "error in the vote tabulation" affected the outcome, it shall conduct a full recount. In the course of the next month, assorted state and federal judges would disagree about whether "error in the vote tabulation" requires a malfunction by the vote-tallying machines or refers more broadly to any failure to register an intended vote—if, for example, on an optical-scan ballot, the voter did not completely fill in the oval with her pencil and the machine did not detect the mark. Or, in the case of punch-card ballots, voters may have indented the space next to a candidate's name but failed to perforate it fully, creating the infamous dimpled and hanging chads. These and related voter failures produced "under-votes." In other cases, a stray pencil mark or other mishap can lead the machine to reject a vote because it detects two—a so-called "over-vote." In either case, a manual recount might reveal the intention of the voter. But the machine's failure to count such ballots resulted from the voter's negligence. Could that be said to constitute an "error in the vote tabulation" as required by Florida law before a full recount is authorized?

Assuming a broad interpretation of "error in the vote tabulation," Gore would have little trouble obtaining a recount. But where? One would think the entire state, but lawyers for Gore and the Florida Democratic Executive Committee exploited loopholes in Florida

election law to request a recount in only four heavily
Democratic counties. These counties accepted the invitation, sampled the requisite 1 percent of ballots, and concluded that a full recount was justified. On November 13,
however, Florida's secretary of state, Katherine Harris,
announced that manual recounts were not lawful and that
she planned to certify the election the following day and
ignore vote totals submitted thereafter. Although she was
an unabashedly partisan Republican, not to mention co-
chair of Bush's campaign in Florida, Harris's position was
not frivolous. She based the November 14 deadline on
state law requiring counties to submit vote counts within
a week of the election. In rejecting recounts, Harris relied
on an advisory opinion by a state agency, the Florida Division of Elections, adopting the restrictive view of "error in the vote tabulation." The director of the Division,
however, was also a loyal Republican with close ties to the
Bush campaign.

In any event, two of the county canvassing boards,
later joined by Gore and the Florida Democratic Party,
filed suit in state court seeking to require Harris to accept
late results based on recounts. The state's Democratic attorney general (who happened to be Gore's state campaign
chairman), Bob Butterworth, issued an advisory opinion
stating that Harris was mistaken and that recounts were
indeed justified. On November 14, four hours prior to
the 5:00 p.m. deadline and Harris's threatened certification, Judge Terry Lewis, ruling on the requested injunc-
tion against Harris, gave a mixed decision that on balance

favored Bush. Judge Lewis held that Harris had the discretion to refuse late-vote count submissions provided she offered some reasonable basis for doing so. She "may not do so arbitrarily," Lewis wrote, setting rather low the bar Harris had to clear to put an end to the recounts.[88]

Judge Lewis's decision was defensible but not obvious, reflecting a problem that plagued the entire process: Under Florida's convoluted election scheme, nothing seemed straightforward. The "error in the vote tabulation" was one of numerous provisions open to multiple interpretations. The code directly contradicted itself with respect to whether the secretary of state could accept late returns: In one section it indicated that she must certify the election seven days following Election Day, but elsewhere indicated that she may opt to extend the deadline. In either case, absentee ballots were not due for ten days after the election, rendering any certification after seven days incomplete. Moreover, a losing candidate could either "protest" or "contest" the election, two distinct actions governed by different time frames and yielding different remedies. The person who best mastered the protest/contest distinction, Gore's lawyer David Boise, used it the way the proverbial drunk uses a lamppost: for support, not illumination. In his book about the case thirteen years later, Charley Wells, the chief justice of the Florida Supreme Court, would lament that most of the lawyers and judges ignored the protest/contest distinction.[89] Bush's attorneys, for their part, insisted that the court stick to the literal text of Florida election law—as if that had a clear meaning. Wells, a self-styled conservative who ended up siding with Bush, acknowledged that the byzantine election code "simply had too many conflicts" to be interpreted in a manner that "met the test of good common sense and logic."[90]

One source of predictability throughout the ordeal was Secretary of State Harris: She favored Bush at every turn. The day after Judge Lewis's decision, Harris reiterated that she would not accept late, revised vote tallies. In response to Lewis's requirement that she offer a reasonable basis for her decision, Harris explained that Gore failed to establish reason to doubt that the pre-recounted vote reflected the will of the voters. Under the circumstances, Harris maintained, the statutory deadline for certification could not be extended short of an act of God or other circumstance beyond the control of the canvassing boards. She announced her intention to wait a few days for the counting of all overseas ballots on November 18, and then certify the election—minus any revised figures other than those of Volusia County, which had already completed its recount and found a net gain of twenty-seven votes for Gore. That knocked Bush's lead down to 300, a tiny difference but one Gore could not possibly make up given Harris's refusal to accept returns based on recounts in the other counties.

The parties returned to Judge Lewis's court on November 16, with Gore's attorneys urging Lewis to prevent Harris from certifying the vote before recounts were completed. At the same time the lawyers argued their case to Lewis, the Florida Supreme Court stepped in to answer a question presented by the Palm Beach canvassing board: Was it permitted to continue with recounts before the secretary of state's decision was litigated? The Court issued an order giving Palm Beach the go-ahead.

The next day, November 17, provided an incomplete victory for Bush. Of the 2,100 overseas ballots counted, he received a net gain of 600, boosting his overall lead in the state to 900. Secretary of State Harris planned, at 5:00 p.m., to certify Bush the winner of the state. Early in the day, she received Judge Lewis's blessing: He upheld Harris's decision to reject late votes with a brief, perfunctory opinion stating that she cleared his low bar by providing a nonarbitrary explanation. Gore immediately appealed Lewis's decision to Florida's Supreme Court, which set the matter for a hearing on November 20. The Court issued a stay forbidding Harris from certifying the state in the interim.

As should be apparent, both sides sought the courts' intervention throughout the recount saga. Whereas Gore requested state court rulings authorizing the recounts, Bush sued in federal court to prevent them. At first blush, Bush's choice of federal court seemed anomalous: Elections are primarily governed by state law and administered by state officials, and Republicans generally lament federal interference with state prerogatives, particularly by the courts. Here, self-interest trumped ideology. Federal litigation figured to end up in the U.S. Supreme Court, where Republican justices predominated.

By contrast, Democratic-appointed judges controlled Florida's Supreme Court. As it turned out, the lawyers for both candidates made the tactically correct call: Gore fared better than Bush in state court and Bush eventually triumphed in federal court, even though his initial foray, urging the U.S. Court of Appeals for the Eleventh Circuit to stop the recounts, was slapped down.

Gore's first significant success in state court occurred on November 21, the day after the hearing before the Florida Supreme Court: The court unanimously reversed Judge Lewis's determination that Secretary of State Harris could certify the state for Bush without awaiting and including recount results. The state's highest court held that "error in the vote tabulation" included any failure to discern an intended vote; it did not require machine malfunction, as Harris maintained. Accordingly, the Court held that Gore was entitled to a recount and that Harris must accept any results completed by November 26. It was not clear where that date came from, and Chief Justice Wells later acknowledged its arbitrariness: The Court sought "a reasonable extended time for voters to have their votes counted" while leaving time for either party to contest the result and for everything to be decided by December 12. (The significance of the latter date is discussed below.) Wells recalled that "the Justices differed substantially as to the new deadline, but all the Justices believed that unanimity was extremely important in this case."[91] The new deadline gave the three remaining counties five days to complete their recount, which figured to be enough. It was Gore's turn to celebrate and Bush's turn to appeal.

Bush immediately sought a writ of certiorari from the U.S. Supreme Court. In the meantime, the recounts proceeded, with Gore gaining votes, particularly in heavily Democratic Miami-Dade. Apparently, many uneducated voters, who overwhelmingly favored Gore, failed to comply perfectly with ballot instructions but made clear the intended beneficiary of their vote. At least that is what Democrats believed. Republicans cried fraud and took the matter into their own hands. On November 22, dozens of GOP operatives and others recruited by them ascended to the nineteenth floor of Miami's Clark Center office tower, where Miami-Dade conducted its recount away from public view and with restricted access for media. The so-called "Brooks Brothers Brigade" produced a "bourgeois riot," screaming and pounding on the door demanding entrance into the room, causing such a disturbance that the canvassing board halted its recount.[92]

On November 26, with Bush maintaining a 537-vote lead, Secretary of State Harris again certified him the winner. She accepted recount results from Broward County but not from Miami-Dade or Palm Beach County, because neither submitted the full results of their recount on time. As noted, Miami-Dade halted its recount midstream in response to on-site protests; Palm Beach submitted the results of its completed recount a few hours after the deadline established by Florida's Supreme Court. The next day, Gore once again filed suit to undo Harris's attempted certification. Meanwhile, on December 1, the U.S. Supreme Court heard oral argument on the Florida Supreme Court's decision to extend the deadline.

The movement in federal court did not halt the simultaneous litigation in state court. On December 2, Florida trial judge Sanders Sauls commenced a two-day hearing to resolve the dispute over Harris's certification. (For those scoring at home, the challenge to an actual certification meant we technically had moved from the "protest" stage to the "contest" stage.) Sauls held that Gore failed to meet the requisite standard for establishing that a recount would change the outcome of the election. While Gore's lawyers easily established that the number of under-votes exceeded Bush's margin, they failed to establish a likelihood that a manual count of these votes would help Gore rather than break even or help Bush. Hence, according to Sauls, Harris was right to certify the state for Bush.

Judge Sauls issued this opinion on December 4, one of two adverse developments for Gore that day. In addition, the U.S. Supreme Court vacated the Florida Supreme Court decision authorizing recounts and extending the deadline for certification, and instructed that Court to clarify the basis of its decision. The U.S. highest court did not decree that Florida's highest court was mistaken, only that the basis for its decision was unclear. In sending the case back for clarification, the U.S. Supreme Court expressed concern that the Florida Supreme Court had essentially rewritten Florida election law, thereby violating

Article II of the U.S. Constitution, which empowers each state's *legislature* to determine the method of selecting electors. It was a remarkable suggestion. On its face, the Florida Supreme Court *interpreted* the scheme created by the state legislature. But it did so in a non-obvious way, which, the U.S. Supreme Court suggested, amounted to improperly changing the election law to accommodate its own ideas of fairness.

In the meantime, following Judge Sauls's adverse ruling, Gore again turned to Florida's Supreme Court. Once again, that court came through for him. On December 8, this time by a 4-3 vote, the state's highest court reversed Sauls's determination that Katherine Harris acted properly in certifying Florida for Bush. The majority found that Judge Sauls held Gore to an overly demanding standard. Gore should have had to show only that there were sufficient uncounted votes "to place in doubt the result of the election."[93] Because Gore easily met this standard, the Court again held that he was entitled to a recount. However, this time the Court clarified that the recount would be in all sixty-seven of the state's counties, not solely in Gore's four handpicked counties. The Court further ordered inclusion of partial recounts in Miami-Dade and Palm Beach, which netted Gore an additional 383 votes, reducing Bush's lead to just 154.

While the Court remedied Gore's cherry-picking, it did not alter another arbitrary aspect of the recount: The canvassing boards were looking for under-votes only, not over-votes. Indeed, the Florida Supreme Court's opinion ordered a statewide recount of under-votes while not mentioning over-votes. One of the dissenting judges, Chief Justice Wells, noted the arbitrary exclusion of over-votes. In addition, Wells cited the absence of a uniform standard for the canvassing boards to apply during their recounts. Noting that the different boards disagreed about numerous questions, such as whether to count a "dimpled chad" as a vote, Wells wrote that "apparently, some do and some do not. Continuation of this system of county-by-county decisions regarding how a dimpled chad is counted is fraught with equal protection concerns."[94] Wells's concern would prove prophetic.

But Wells's colleagues outvoted him and reversed Judge Sauls. The Court sent the case back to Sauls, who opted to recuse himself without explanation. The Florida Supreme Court had assessed his opinion in unflattering terms, and perhaps Sauls felt that the insult rendered it inappropriate for him to remain on the case. Whatever his reason, the recusal was odd. Trial judges routinely handle cases on remand following reversal by a higher court. Indeed, when Sauls disqualified himself, the case was reassigned to Judge Terry Lewis, who had also been reversed by the Florida Supreme Court during the post-election litigation.

Lewis immediately commenced hearings to determine a standard for evaluating ballots during the recount. He focused on an issue that received extensive media attention and complaints from Republicans: dimpled and hanging chads on punch-card ballots. Judge

Lewis seemed eager to establish a single standard across the state, but the parties could not agree on a standard, and Lewis ultimately declined to impose one. He left it up to the canvassing boards, while making himself available to resolve disputes. Lewis ordered that recounts be completed by 2:00 p.m. on December 12, the so-called "safe harbor" date—the federal provision (adopted by the Electoral Count Act in the aftermath of the 1876 election) establishing that Congress must accept any electoral votes submitted within six days of the convening of the Electoral College (which, in 2000, was December 18). That gave the canvassing boards four days to do the job.

However, on the next day, December 9, the U.S. Supreme Court issued a "stay" stopping the recounts pending its decision on their legality. The Court scheduled oral argument for December 11. The overlapping state and federal court proceedings created confusion. As noted, four days before the Florida Supreme Court's *second* ruling, a unanimous U.S. Supreme Court vacated the *first* decision by Florida's Supreme Court and asked the Florida court to explain whether it had interpreted state law or come up with its own. The court had not responded to that unusual request, and on December 11, during oral argument in the case appealing the second Florida Supreme Court decision, Justice Sandra Day O'Connor criticized the state court for not responding. The Florida Supreme Court scrambled to draft and release its response later that day. Unsurprisingly, the state court took the hint from above and clarified that it had based its decision on its reading of Florida election law.

This was important, because the U.S. Supreme Court has no jurisdiction over matters of state law unless the law or court decision in question violates federal law, including the U.S. Constitution. However, the Supreme Court nevertheless reversed the Florida Supreme Court's second decision (the one delivered on December 8 but "stayed" on December 9, as the Florida Supreme Court's first decision was now moot). In a decision handed down on December 12, the Court held that the recounts violated the U.S. Constitution. To be clear, six justices took the Florida Supreme Court at its word that it had indeed interpreted the state election code rather than simply making things up and usurping the power given to the legislature by Article II of the U. S. Constitution. Justices Scalia, Rehnquist, and Thomas issued a concurring opinion claiming otherwise, but they were two votes short of the necessary majority. However, seven justices found a different violation of the U.S. Constitution—one that seemed odd in several respects.

Picking up on Chief Justice Wells's dissent from the Florida Supreme Court decision, the Court observed that the state court's decision did not articulate a standard for canvassing boards to apply. In the recounts that had taken place to date, different precincts used different standards for determining what counted as a vote. To take the main example, some canvassing boards considered dimpled and hanging chads sufficient to indicate a voter's intent, others counted hanging but not dimpled chads, and still others counted neither. In addition, the Court echoed Wells's complaint that the canvassing boards looked only for under-votes and ignored over-votes. Seven justices of the U.S. Supreme Court (all but Ginsburg and Stevens) believed that these discrepancies in the treatment of ballots by the different canvassing boards violated the Fourteenth Amendment's guarantee of equal protection under the law.

One problem with the Court's ruling was its apparent stunning breadth. If different standards for determining votes violated equal protection, then the entire election, not just in Florida but nationwide, was one big equal protection violation (and countless little ones). Different precincts, both within states and from state to state, used different methods for counting and, if necessary, recounting ballots. Why was the Court suddenly committed to uniformity?[95]

Indeed, the Court recognized that its equal protection ruling would have extraordinary repercussions for elections everywhere. Accordingly, the Court's main opinion (which five justices joined but none would acknowledge authoring, instead issuing it *per curiam*, meaning "by the court") included a most unusual sentence: "Our consideration is limited to the present circumstances, for the problem of equal protection in election processes generally presents many complexities."[96] It is rare, if not unprecedented, for a Court to advise that its ruling should never be followed in future cases.[97]

This striking statement reinforced a fundamental

problem with the Supreme Court's decision: Five conservative justices, who normally interpret equal protection narrowly and states' rights broadly, jettisoned their long-held convictions. Was it a coincidence that such inconsistency, if not hypocrisy, enabled them to dictate that the next president would be one to their liking? Had they latched onto an argument they didn't believe in because they needed to guarantee George W. Bush's victory? Many people, including some Republicans, found the equal protection argument flabbergasting.[98]

There was one more problem still with the Court's equal protection ruling. It followed from the ruling that, to escape the equal protection violation, Florida's Supreme Court would have had to establish a single standard for the recounts across the state. However, the U.S. Supreme Court had already put the state court on notice that it could not alter the statutory scheme without violating Article II's stipulation that the state *legislature* determines how electors are selected. With the benefit of hindsight, we can see that the U.S. Supreme Court placed the Florida Supreme Court in an untenable position: Allow each precinct to determine how to conduct the recount and you violate equal protection, but establish a uniform standard and you violate Article II. This bind amounts to the U.S. Supreme Court saying that 1) the Florida legislature established an unconstitutional method for recounts, but 2) it could not be changed. This logic works only under the assumption that the Court was determined to prevent recounts—period.

Notwithstanding all of the above, the Court's ruling on equal protection was defensible. Equal protection does require, at a minimum, that government actions be rational and serve some legitimate purpose. Does it make sense to have dimpled chads count as a vote in one county and not another? In fact, the Court's equal protection ruling commanded *seven* votes, including two by progressive justices, Breyer and Souter. However, Justices Breyer and Souter did *not* believe the recounts should be stopped. Since Florida law did provide for recounts (as affirmed by the Florida Supreme Court, in a decision that six justices on the U.S. Supreme Court accepted), the obvious solution was to do what higher courts routinely do when they identify a constitutional problem: send it back to the lower court to see if it could be fixed. In this case, Justices Breyer and Souter maintained, Florida's Supreme Court, or some official designated by that court, could establish a uniform standard for the statewide recount, thereby curing the equal protection problem.

The five conservative justices said no, for a simple reason: There wasn't time. The federal law adopted in the aftermath of the 1876 presidential election fiasco dictates that for a state's electoral votes to be automatically accepted by Congress, the slate of electors must be determined and certified six days before the Electoral College meets in person. In 2000, the Electoral College was set to meet on December 18, making December 12 the so-called "safe harbor" date. However, the Supreme Court handed down its decision at 10:00 p.m. on December 12! Because no timely recount was possible, the Court said, the secretary of state's certification must stand. Bush would receive Florida's electoral votes, and hence the presidency. The next day, Gore conceded for the second and final time.

There were several disturbing aspects of the Court's ruling with respect to the lack of time for a recount. First, the relevant federal provision that established the safe harbor in no way *required* that a state's electoral votes be submitted by December 12. That date merely ties the hands of Congress when it comes to accepting such. States remained free to get the votes certified at any time before December 18, when the Electoral College convened, and there was no reason to think Congress would not accept them as late as that date. As Justice Breyer wrote in dissent, "Whether there is time to conduct a recount prior to December 18 . . . is a matter for the state courts to decide."[99]

The *Bush v. Gore* Court offered an ingenious but disingenuous response on this point: As a matter of *Florida law*, they said, ballots must be in by December 12. However, the only basis for that conclusion was a reference to the safe harbor in one of the Florida Supreme Court opinions in this case. The Florida Supreme Court indicated that it would be desirable, even expected, for the state's electors to be determined by that date, but it in no way said that this was *required* or trumps the value of more accurate results reflected in a recount. Even Professor Michael McConnell, a conservative who approved the other aspects of the U.S. Supreme Court's opinion, rejected the Court's decision to stop the counting based on the safe harbor as a deadline.[100]

The depressing irony is that the alleged safe harbor requirement was the single point about which the U.S. Supreme Court deferred to the Florida Supreme Court's interpretation of Florida law—deferring to something the five conservative justices conjured up and used as a basis for defeating the central contentions of the Florida Supreme Court: that Gore and Florida voters were entitled to a recount and that such a recount could and should take place.[101] Again, the U.S. Court could have followed the usual path and remanded the case to the Florida Supreme Court to determine whether, under Florida law, December 12 is indeed a decisive date. But the U.S. Supreme Court wasn't taking any chances.

In this connection, the five conservative Justices made another staggering statement. Noting that Justices Breyer and Souter agreed with them that the recounts violated equal protection, they stated that "the only disagreement is as to the remedy."[102] The *only* disagreement? As the macabre joke goes, "Besides that Mrs. Lincoln, how did you like the play?"

There was one additional egregious aspect to this disheartening business. One reason there was no time to complete recounts is that the Supreme Court, three days earlier, issued a stay halting the recounts. Such rare action requires the party seeking the stay to show that it would suffer "irreparable harm" absent such a stay. In other words, Bush had to show that if the recounts were allowed to continue, but later declared improper, it would be too late to undo the damage to him. But why? Assuming the recount led to an apparent Gore victory, the decision to undo the recount could have occurred before the Electoral College met, and certainly before Congress made the tally official. Bush would become president. What "irreparable" harm would he suffer?

In granting the stay, Justice Scalia offered two sources of such harm. First, if the recount proceeded, ballots might become "degraded," thus distorting a later recount (in case the Court held that the first recount was invalid but a new one should proceed). This argument, which almost no one defended or repeated, does not pass the giggle test. Scalia's slightly more serious argument was that, if the recount went forward and Gore appeared to win, but the recount was later declared invalid and Bush became president, this state of affairs risked "casting a cloud upon what [Bush] claims to be the legitimacy of the election."[103]

Invoking this capacious notion of irreparable harm, Scalia came close to admitting that he saw his role as protecting Bush's political prospects. After all, and as Justice Stevens noted in his dissent from the stay, Scalia ignored the far greater and truly irreparable harm to Gore of stopping the recount when time was of the essence. As Stevens said (prophetically, as it turned out), granting the stay was "tantamount to a decision on the merits" favoring Bush.[104] For even if the Court later found that the recounts should proceed, there might be insufficient time for them—exactly what happened, albeit partly because the Court favored Bush in a second improbable respect, insisting that December 12 was the final day for recounts to be completed.

To be sure, the issuing of the stay turned out to be irrelevant to the outcome of the case. Had the stay not been issued, and the recounts continued from December 9 to 12, the Court's equal protection ruling on December 12 would have invalidated some or all of the recounting. Thus, at least given the Court's insistence on December 12 as the final deadline for votes to be submitted, there still would have been no time for the statewide recount. However, it is possible that Gore would have taken the lead in the interim, and the Court's decision would then have *seemed* even more result-oriented than it did. As a matter of public relations, both Bush's win and the Court itself might indeed be somewhat tainted. But, again, such concerns veer far from the traditional notion of irreparable harm. The stay protected Bush, and to a lesser extent the Court itself, but that was a problem rather than a solution.

While I believe that the Supreme Court's handiwork in *Bush v. Gore* was outrageous, it does not follow that a manual recount made much sense. For one thing, even though the recount probably could have been completed by December 18, it seems unlikely that the six-day period would have sufficed for both sides to contest canvassing boards' determinations, with recourse to the courts for adjudication of disputes.[105] That said, this decision should have been left to Florida courts. But a more compelling argument against recounts came from a statistician, John Allen Paulos, in a *New York Times* op-ed. Discerning the true winner in an election producing a virtual tie among 6 million voters is simply impossible, Paulos observed, akin to "measuring bacteria with a yardstick."[106] And why stop at one recount when another would almost certainly produce a different count and quite possibly a different outcome? Or, as Florida's Supreme Court chief justice Charles Wells put it (in a book thirteen years later), no matter how many times the votes were counted, "the margin of error was always going to be greater than the margin of victory."[107]

A media consortium later examined the ballots state-wide and determined that the real winner was . . . it depends. Under certain standards for counting votes, Bush would have won; under other standards, Gore. In almost all scenarios, the margin was ridiculously tiny. And, of course, actual recounts would have been undertaken by different people in different circumstances from the no-pressure counting by the media consortium.[108]

After the consortium made public its findings, supporters of both candidates again claimed victory, but the real truth was this: We have no idea which candidate received more votes in Florida. Whatever statewide standard became adopted would have been arbitrary and yet decisive. In the end, we may have been better off sticking to the first result—the Election Day tally modified by the automatic machine recount and inclusion of absentee ballots from overseas. That was the only one that was determined before canvassing board members became involved, and made subjective decisions knowing that the entire presidential election stood in the balance.

In seeking a solution to future presidential election crises, we must keep in mind the numerous phenomena that can interfere with a fair outcome. Florida in 2000 displayed many. We've already alluded to a few—poorly designed ballots and indirect voter suppression—that weren't the focus of the litigation over the election. We can add a complaint waged by Bush supporters that also did not lend itself to a remedy. When the networks originally called the state for Gore, polls remained open in the state's so-called panhandle—Republican territory. Conceivably, the network's projection discouraged would-be Bush voters from showing up to vote.

Additional issues arose from the absentee-ballot process. First, evidence established that some local officials responded differently to Republican and Democratic voters who applied for absentees.[109] Second, some 680 absentee ballots, some from members of the military abroad, did not comply with Florida law. Many were not postmarked or dated and signed by Election Day, or failed to meet some other requirement such as the signature of a witness. However, Florida law, as interpreted by its courts, requires only "substantial compliance" with such rules. For public relations reasons (it looks bad to exclude votes from soldiers), Gore chose not to contest those votes, even though Bush received a vastly disproportionate number of them. We find here another reminder of the impossibility of determining the "real winner" when a large state like Florida produces a virtual tie.

Another major lesson from the 2000 election concerns the Supreme Court's regrettable involvement. Even if the Court arrived at the correct decision in stopping the recounts, it did so for the wrong reasons, calling to mind T.S. Eliot's aphorism that "the greatest treason" consists of "the right deed for the wrong reason."[110] We do well to dwell on the wrong reasons for the Court's *Bush v. Gore* decision, because doing so reinforces a crucial truth connecting the 2000 presidential election to its 1876 precursor: A partisan court deciding elections is no better than a partisan ad hoc commission—or partisan officials of any kind."[111]

The Supreme Court recognized the perils of getting involved, noting defensively that resolving the dispute was its "unsought responsibility."[112] This was an odd remark. The Court *never* seeks responsibility to resolve a dispute, because it has no authority to do so: It cannot become involved in a case absent a party's legal filing invoking the Court's jurisdiction. Moreover, while Bush asked the Court to take the case, it easily could have declined to do so. The Court refuses to hear most cases, and nothing about this case required that it be taken. Indeed, as many commentators have noted, the case arguably fell within the "political question" doctrine under which courts decline to decide a case because Congress and/or the president is better situated to resolve the matter.[113]

Had the Supreme Court stayed out, and Bush won

after the recounts, questions of his (and the Court's) legitimacy would have been avoided. Had Gore won, in all likelihood the Republican-controlled Florida legislature would have intervened. If it did so, and the result was competing sets of electors sent to Congress, the winner would have been determined by the United States Congress (the body charged with counting and recording electoral votes). The Florida legislature and U.S. Congress are accountable to voters.[114] How ironic that the Supreme Court's decision to take the case in the first place, and then to resolve it rather than remand it to Florida to do so, was made by conservative justices who, as a matter of judicial philosophy, usually insist that courts defer to the democratic processes. Moreover, had the Florida legislature or U.S. Congress acted unconstitutionally, the Court could have intervened *then*. To short-circuit the process served Bush's short-term interests but arguably harmed the Court and country, and certainly veered from the philosophy of those who imposed this resolution.

The Court's seemingly gratuitous plea of "unsought responsibility" reflected its accurate anticipation that it would be accused of handing Bush the presidency. To take one of numerous examples, *The New Republic* titled its cover story on the case "The Supreme Court Commits Suicide."[115] The Court survived, but Justice Stevens's dissent captured the cost of its intervention: "Although we may never know with complete certainty the identity of the winner of this year's Presidential election, the identity of the loser is perfectly clear. It is the Nation's confidence in the judge as an impartial guardian of the rule of law."[116]

The Court's costly involvement illuminates the larger point that we still lack a fruitful mechanism for deciding disputed presidential elections. In 1876, the Supreme Court indirectly determined that Hayes was the winner when Justice Bradley cast the deciding vote on the ad hoc commission; in 2000, the Court made the choice more directly. In each case, the losing side justifiably felt that it had been deprived of a fair shake. It might be different if Supreme Court justices were considered truly impartial. But they aren't, and, in part because of cases like *Bush v. Gore*, they won't be any time soon. The almost circular reasoning here actually makes sense: If we want to promote the legitimacy of both the Supreme Court and the White House, we should not allow the Court to pick the president.[117]

One final irony warrants mention, because it, too, underscores the inadequacy of current procedures for resolving disputed elections. Suppose Al Gore had not conceded, but instead followed the advice of some of his lawyers and petitioned the Florida Supreme Court to act, following the U.S. Supreme Court decision holding that there was insufficient time to conduct the recount. Imagine that the Florida Supreme Court held that the U.S. Supreme Court misread its interpretation of state law, and that recounts could continue until December 18. Now suppose that recounts proceeded and Gore won. As occurred in 1876, when Congress met to finalize the results, it would have had in its hands two competing certifications of Florida's electors. The person constitutionally authorized to open the certificates, and perhaps responsible for resolving disputes, is the president of the Senate—meaning the vice president of the United States. Which was . . . Al Gore.

That would have been just one more wrinkle in an election that taught us how many problems can afflict an election. The issues that affected Florida are worth recapping. Before a single ballot was cast, voter suppression may have compromised the legitimacy of the election. On Election Day, a poorly designed ballot led a few thousand voters to cast a vote contrary to their intentions. Numerous absentee ballots did not conform to statutory standards. Many thousands of voters were effectively disenfranchised when, through some combination of their own negligence and the failure of machines, their vote was not counted. This problem could have been remedied by a manual recount, but such a recount was itself fraught with problems, including: 1) ambiguity in the state's election code concerning the necessity, timing, and/or scope of any recount; 2) absence of a statewide standard for recounts; and 3) disagreement over whether that disparity violated the U.S. Constitution. These and other complex issues occupied state and federal courts, which were hamstrung by suspicion of bias and the need to act hastily.

By fluke, all of these things came together in a state that happened to be tied and determinative of the national election outcome. We can be confident that we will not again experience anything quite like Florida 2000. But in terms of all the circumstances that can complicate presidential elections, Florida was more warning than outlier. As Professor Richard Epstein says, Florida "highlighted this soft underbelly of American elections, just as it threw into high relief the peculiar operations of our electoral college."[118]

Of the countless commentaries about *Bush v. Gore*, perhaps the least contestable summary was supplied by Yale Law School Professor Stephen Carter:

> The one thing of which I am absolutely sure is that had Gore—rather than Bush—won the second count, only to face a Florida Supreme Court order for a third, it would have been the Gore campaign that appealed to the Supreme Court to intervene, and the Bush campaign arguing feverishly in favor of letting the state's process go forward. No principle was involved on either side, except the principle that says my guy ought to win.[119]

Alas, Carter's observation applies with equal force to many of the judges as well as the lawyers, not to mention many members of the media and the general public. That no one can be trusted to rise above self-interest in such matters is one of the crucial lessons of *Bush v. Gore*.

The almost universal displeasure with the way things

played out in the thirty-six days after Election Day 2000 led to widespread call for reform. Private groups created a bipartisan National Commission on Federal Election Reform, chaired by ex-presidents Ford and Carter, to make recommendations. The commission's report captured the global nature of the problem: "Everyone who observed the 2000 election crisis was struck by the sheer unreadiness of every part of the system to deal with a close election."[120] The commission's recommendations spurred Congress to enact the Help America Vote Act (HAVA), which, among other things, prohibited punch-card voting (no more hanging chads!), set forth requirements for all voting systems, provided funding to replace outdated machines, mandated that "provisional ballots" be given to voters whose eligibility is questioned at the polls, and established an Election Assistance Commission. President Bush signed the measure into law in 2002.

Despite the authors' claim that the report's recommendations solve "most of the problems that came into national view" in 2000, and despite the report's reassuring title—"To Assure Pride and Confidence in the Electoral Process"—HAVA does little to prevent future mishaps. Indeed, as elections law expert Professor Edward Foley shrewdly observed, it could have made things worse in the very next presidential election. In 2004, the entire election once again hinged on a single exceptionally close state (Ohio). Not close enough, it turned out, to require a recount and threaten a reprise of 2000. But, as Professor Foley pointed out, had Ohio been a little closer, HAVA would have made things more rather than less chaotic: "The provisional ballots that Congress in HAVA had just mandated . . . would have been the obvious target of opportunity for eager litigators waiting to pounce."[121]

There were more than 158,000 such ballots in Ohio, so any fight over them would have been protracted. But perhaps the key word in Foley's analysis is "litigators." HAVA did nothing to keep presidential elections out of court, nor to reduce the time pressure that courts (and canvassing boards tasked with recounts) will operate under. Professor Foley, again: "Ohio was a near-miss scare, akin to the doomsday scenario that comes frighteningly close. . . . [Had Ohio been a little closer] there would have been litigation in both state and federal courts over whether or not to count particular provisional ballots, and the U.S. Supreme Court would have been asked to weigh in. One need not concoct hypotheticals to realize what a nightmare it would have been."[122]

The other major criticism of HAVA concerns an error of omission. As its title—Help America Vote Act—implies, the legislation focused on making elections smoother and fairer, which could reduce the likelihood of a disputed election. But HAVA did nothing to assist in the resolution of disputed elections that do occur. In other words, it did not provide the means of preventing disputes from morphing into crises à la 1876 and 2000.

Significant action should be taken to reduce the vulnerabilities of our presidential elections *before* the next crisis. I propose such measures in the final two chapters.

FIVE

NEAR CRISIS, NEXT CRISIS: THE ELECTION OF 2016 AND BEYOND

While we may never learn the full extent of the covert attempts to infiltrate and manipulate the 2016 U.S. presidential election, what we do know should alarm if not terrify us. A National Security Agency report published seven months after the election concluded that "Russian intelligence obtained and maintained access to elements of multiple U.S. state or local electoral boards."[123] Two years later, Special Counsel Robert Mueller's long-awaited report confirmed that Russians undertook this and other actions in order to help Donald Trump win the White House. Among other things, the Russians manipulated social media to spread disinformation and disseminated private emails hacked from Clinton campaign chairman, John Podesta, and other leading Democrats.

Revelations subsequent to the Mueller report are

even more disturbing. The Senate Intelligence Committee issued a bipartisan report concluding that, during the 2016 election, Russia breached election systems in all fifty states, an attack "more far-reaching than previously acknowledged and one largely undetected by the states and federal officials at the time."[124] The Senate report was released less than twenty-four hours after Mueller warned that Russia is moving forward with plans to interfere in future elections.

While the Senate investigation found that the Russian government "directed extensive activity . . . against U.S. election infrastructure at the state and local level,"[125] there have been no disclosures of attempts to interfere with the actual casting or tabulating of votes. However, we cannot rule out that possibility. Indeed, the heavily redacted Senate report implied that the Russians, among others, may be currently seeking means of altering votes in future elections, and that outdated voting machines in many states remain particularly susceptible to such efforts. The report quotes Dr. Alex Halderman, a professor of computer science at the University of Michigan, as saying that "our highly computerized election infrastructure is vulnerable to sabotage and even cyberattacks that could change votes."[126] Some experts speculate that hackers—including foreign governments—already have the ability to alter votes in our voting machines.

The Cybersecurity Infrastructure Security Agency, a division of the Homeland Security Department, is also concerned that election systems could become paralyzed by ransomware, a type of cyberattack that has already sabotaged municipal computer networks in Baltimore, Atlanta and other cities.[127] "This threat to our democracy will not go away, and concern about ransomware attacks on voter registration databases is one clear example," said Vermont Secretary of State Jim Condos.[128] "A pre-election undetected attack could tamper with voter lists, creating huge confusion and delays, disenfranchisement, and at large enough scale could compromise the validity of the election," according to John Sebes, a chief officer at the OSET (Open Source Election Technology) Institute, an election technology policy think tank.[129]

In addition to sabotage and extortion, we must beware of efforts by foreign and domestic entities to spread disinformation or weaponize hacked data. Such activities are particularly dangerous because they may provide leverage against the president they help elect. But, unless the president or members of his or her campaign participate in such activities, or at least know about them and fail to alert the authorities, they do not call into question the legitimacy of an election. Vote tampering obviously crosses that line. If a president engages in or knows of such activities and doesn't report them, he or she should be impeached and removed. Whether or not the candidate knows about it in advance, if enough votes are tampered with to affect the outcome of the election, the election is a sham and the "winner's" claim to office lacks legitimacy.

In 2016, even minimal vote tampering could have changed the outcome of the election. To be sure, although Trump received millions fewer votes than Hillary Clinton, his victory in the Electoral College was reasonably comfortable: He received seventy-seven more electoral votes than Clinton, a margin exceeding that of twelve presidential winners. But Trump's seventy-seven vote Electoral College victory is less impressive than it might seem. This misleadingly large margin stems from a combination of two factors: the winner-take-all nature of the Electoral College and the fact that Trump won several sizable states by a tiny amount. His margin over Clinton in Michigan, Pennsylvania, and Wisconsin was less than 1 percent, and in Florida just 1.2 percent. Had Clinton won those four states, she would have received 302 electoral votes to Trump's 229—almost a perfect reversal of Trump's victory (304–227). Clinton also won a few states by tiny margins, but they happened to be small states with far fewer electoral votes.

As we shall see in the next chapter, 2016 was not an outlier: The Electoral College often produces results where a small swing of votes in a few states would have yielded a different winner. This point is particularly salient with respect to 2016, however, because a foreign power covertly engaged in substantial activity to manipulate the outcome.

Though no evidence suggests that attacks by Russians or other malicious actors affected the actual casting or tabulation of votes, it is important to recognize that even a little bit of such chicanery can easily affect the result of an election. We will never know whether the Russians' weaponization of social media and other covert operations got Trump over the top, but perhaps next time the Russians will not rely on indirect efforts: Next time they—or someone else—may engage in vote tampering. No one puts it past them to try, and there is no reason to assume they could not succeed.

In September 2018, an annual hacker conference simulated an election utilizing actual election equipment and created a "Voting Machine Hacking Village" that successfully breached every piece of voting machinery.[130] The people who organized the conference drafted a lengthy report that issued the following conclusions:

> • A voting tabulator currently used in 23 states is vulnerable to remote hacking via a network attack. Because the device in question is a high-speed unit designed to process a high volume of ballots for an entire county, hacking just one of these machines could enable an attacker to flip the Electoral College and determine the outcome of a presidential election.

> • A second critical vulnerability in the same machine was disclosed to the vendor a decade ago, yet that machine, which was used into 2016, still contains the flaw.

> • Another machine used in 18 states was hacked in only two minutes, while it takes the average

voter six minutes to vote. Thus one could hack a voting machine on Election Day within the time it takes to vote.

• Hackers had the ability to wirelessly repro-gram, via mobile phone, a type of electronic card used by millions of Americans to activate the voting terminal to cast their ballots. This vulnerability could be exploited to take over the voting machine and cast as many votes as the voter wanted. [131]

The report's conclusions dovetail with what experts have been telling us. In the book *Hacking Elections Is Easy*, the authors, experts on cyber-security, explain that, well, hacking elections is easy: "The Question is not, 'Are script kiddies, lone-wolves, hacktivists, cyber-mercenar-ies, or nation-state actors from Russia or China trying to impact our elections? Rather, due to our virtually de-fenseless election process, the questions that should be asked are, 'Why wouldn't they?' and 'How do we know that they have not already done so?'"[132]

Lest this be seen as alarmist, note that the National Academy of Sciences, Engineering, and Medicine concurs that our elections are extremely vulnerable. They observe that malware (malicious software that creates viruses and the like) "can be introduced at any point in the electronic path of a vote—from the software behind the vote-casting interface to the software tabulating votes—to prevent a voter's vote from being recorded as intended."[133]

The threat of a presidential election undermined by foreign interference has grown to the point that the FBI has publicly warned about it and actively works to safeguard against it.[134] (Alas, the same cannot be said for the Senate, which has refused to vote on critical election security bills.)[135] Meanwhile, the *New York Times* reports that "intelligence officials believe Russia intends to raise questions in the aftermath of future elections about irregularities or purported fraud to undermine faith in the result."[136] But would Russia settle for raising questions about irregularities or fraud if they can do the real thing, taking action that actually doctors results? As noted, we cannot rule out the possibility that this occurred in 2016. The FBI determined that a Russian military intelligence unit hacked into voter registration systems in Florida, which could have enabled them to delete or add voters to the rolls and cancel mail-in ballots.[137] Needless to say, such activities can affect the actual vote count. Department of Homeland Security officials have declared themselves "confident" that the activities in Florida had no impact on vote totals, but confidence is not certainty.[138]

Because there is no evidence that any hackers actually affected the tabulation of votes, we may be lulled into a false sense of security. That is, we may not be asking, at least with sufficient urgency, what would happen if Russia or some other force directly compromises our election.

Consider a thought experiment involving an alternate history of the 2016 election. Suppose the Mueller report found that the Russians had successfully hacked the vote-counting machinery in Michigan and Pennsylvania, switching enough votes to change the outcome of the election. (Note that Trump won Michigan and Pennsylvania by just 55,000 votes combined.) Were it not for the Russian operations, according to our hypothetical investigation, Clinton would have won these states and therefore the presidency. Had this happened, a few days later we might have awakened to something like the following news report.

Revelations that Russia essentially hijacked our election naturally outraged Democrats. Many, including Speaker of the House Nancy Pelosi, are calling for President Trump's impeachment. Most legal scholars, however, believe that impeachment is inappropriate unless it can be demonstrated that Trump, or at least members of his campaign, knew about the Russian effort.

Other Democrats are demanding that Trump and Vice President Mike Pence resign, to be replaced by Clinton and her running mate, Senator Tim Kaine. But this approach, too, appears to lack a legal basis. The Constitution provides that Congress shall determine the line of succession governing vacancies in the offices of both president and vice president. Congress long ago established that next in line is the Speaker of the House— in this case, Ms. Pelosi.

Harvard Law School professor Laurence Tribe, a constitutional law expert, notes that "the whole line of succession is laid out in federal law. In the event of double vacancy the Speaker of the House becomes president, followed by the president pro tempore of the Senate. After that, it's the secretary of state and cabinet members all the way down."

Tribe is counseling Democrats that there is nevertheless a path to a Clinton-Kaine administration. "As soon as Pelosi takes office, she should nominate Clinton as vice president. After the Senate confirms Clinton, Pelosi resigns and Clinton becomes president. Clinton then nominates Kaine to the vice presidency to fill that vacancy."

The major obstacle to Professor Tribe's scenario is Republican control of the Senate. Senate Majority Leader Mitch McConnell says he foresees no circumstances in which members of his caucus would vote to confirm Ms. Clinton as vice president. And all such speculation may be moot given that Trump apparently has no intention of resigning. White House communications director Sarah Sanders put out a statement that leaves little room for interpretation.

"It will be a cold day in hell before President Trump and Vice President Pence resign the office so that Nancy Pelosi or anyone else can become president."

A bipartisan group of Democratic and Republican lawmakers has huddled to consider legislation calling for a special election, presumably pitting Clinton and Trump in a rematch. However, this idea is already under attack from both sides of the aisle.

"This is not a tennis match, best two out of three sets," Senate Minority leader Chuck Schumer said. "Hillary won the election, and we must find a way to make her president."

"If Democrats don't like the results of this election, there's another one in less than two years," McConnell said.

What about the fact that, according to the Mueller report, the election had been stolen by a foreign country?

"That's just speculation," McConnell said. "And it wouldn't matter if it was stone cold fact. There's nothing in the Constitution authorizing a special election. If you don't like it, move to Europe. You'll get all the special elections you want over there."

McConnell was asked whether he would say the same thing if a Democrat had won the White House thanks to a foreign nation switching votes away from the Republican candidate.

"What I would say makes no difference," McConnell said. "What matters is what the Constitution says. If people don't like the Constitution, they can amend it."

This alternative history is not far-fetched. Had the Russians—or anyone else—made Trump president by tampering with votes, and had the discovery of the chicanery been made only after Trump's inauguration, something like the scenario sketched above likely would have transpired. Moreover, the sentiment attributed to Mitch McConnell is correct: The Constitution does *not* provide means for undoing an improper presidential election.

Spanish philosopher José Ortega y Gasset has observed, "The health of any democracy, no matter what its type or status, depends on a small technical detail: the conduct of elections."[139] And U.S. law professor Robert Bennett notes, "Selection of the president is the single most important and gripping event in American democracy. . . . There is no more serious concern we should have about American democracy than that the process of selection may work very badly."[140]

The 2016 election reminds us that, notwithstanding the ample warnings provided by the elections of 1800, 1824, 1876, and 2000, we have done little to fix the problems plaguing presidential elections. As noted, it is a certainty that Russian covert operations attacked the 2016 election, and in July 2019, Robert Mueller testified that Russia continues efforts to sabotage our system.[141] In October 2019, the Associated Press reported that "hackers linked to the Iranian government targeted a U.S. presidential campaign, as well as government officials, media targets and prominent expatriate Iranians."[142] It is a near certainty that numerous entities will intensify efforts to infiltrate voting systems and determine future election outcomes. Accordingly, several questions demand immediate answers. What can we do to reduce the likelihood of the scenario in which the wrong candidate (meaning one who receives fewer legitimate electoral votes than their opponent) is deemed the winner? If this dangerous scenario does in fact come to pass, do we have a means of redressing it? If not, what can we do to establish such means? The next two chapters take up these questions.

SIX

THE ELECTORAL COLLEGE: A RECIPE FOR FRAUD AND CHAOS

The presidential election crises in 1800, 1824, 1876, and 2000 each resulted from its own set of causes. The 1800 fiasco resulted from a quirk in the Constitution that produced a tie between running mates, the 1824 crisis stemmed from multiple viable candidates, and the 1876 donnybrook came about due to negligence and corruption. In 2000, the stars aligned perversely: The election hinged on a virtual tie in a state with poor voting machinery and convoluted recount procedures, among other problems. These various election disputes were also resolved through different means: in 1800 and 1824, by the House of Representatives; in 1876, by an ad hoc commission; and in 2000 by the United States Supreme Court.[143] Historians debate whether these outcomes were legitimate, but, with the exception of 1800, each outcome undeniably left the losing party feeling robbed.

The other presidential election we have considered, that of 2016, produced a potential crisis stemming from yet another source—covert foreign operations designed to assist one candidate. Though crisis was averted, because (unlike in the aforementioned elections) one candidate clearly received the most electoral votes and there was no evidence of vote tampering, here too the losing candidate and her supporters were understandably chagrined by the circumstances surrounding her defeat.

One other common thread runs through these disparate elections: In each, the crisis—or potential crisis, in the case of 2016—stemmed in part from the Electoral College, a result not entirely unforeseeable. Whatever virtues the Electoral College may have (as discussed below), it does not assure an orderly election. In a piece written just before Election Day in 2000, Professor Akhil Amar prophetically remarked on the "outside chance of a constitutional meltdown in the days ahead."[144] Amar did not have in mind a virtual tie (followed by a battle royale over recounts) but rather an *actual* tie—each candidate receiving 269 electoral votes.[145] Still, if Amar narrowly missed prophesying the precise crisis that was days away, he nailed the larger point: Severe potential problems may arise from "the Constitution's archaic and confusing rules concerning the Electoral College."[146]

The most common complaint about the Electoral College is its risk of negating the votes of millions of American citizens, and installing a person as president who receives fewer votes than his or her opponent. In four elections discussed earlier—1824, 1876, 2000, 2016—the candidate who won the presidency lost the popular vote, an event that also occurred in 1888. This fact alone delegitimized these five elections in the eyes of many, although the risk of a divergence between the popular vote and Electoral College vote had once seemed too improbable to be terribly worrisome. (In that sense, the "wrong winner" was akin to the "faithless elector" who ignores the vote in their own state—a theoretical problem not worth fretting over.) The fact that the Electoral College winner lost the popular vote twice in the last five elections gives the discussion more urgency. And it must not be thought that 2000 and 2016 were fluky. On the contrary, the real surprise is that the Electoral College and popular vote diverged so infrequently before 2000.

That this would change was not only foreseeable, but foreseen. In a prescient analysis written in 1996, Lawrence Longley and Neal Peirce warned that we could be headed down this path: "Careful analysis shows that the danger of an Electoral College misfire is not just historical but immediate in any close contest. In fact, only sheer luck in several recent elections has saved the nation from the electoral college victory of the popular vote loser."[147] Twenty years later, we were taken by surprise by the sharpest divergence ever between the Electoral College and popular vote, with Hillary Clinton losing the former by seventy-seven votes despite winning the latter by almost three million votes. We would have been less surprised if we had heeded Longley and Peirce, who, based on statistical analysis, warned that a popular vote winner by 2 million to 3 million votes would still lose the Electoral College roughly 25 percent of the time.

It is misleading, however, to assume that the "wrong" candidate wins (or that the Electoral College "misfired") when he or she loses the popular vote. The rules were clear beforehand, and the candidates sought victory in the Electoral College, not in the popular vote. The candidates surely would have campaigned differently had the winner been determined by popular vote. To employ a much-used analogy, the candidate who wins the presidency while losing the popular vote is arguably no less legitimate than the World Series champion that was outscored by its opponent in total runs. Total runs is a meaningless category, analogous to total votes within an election governed by the Electoral College.[148] Baseball has always has been operated as a series of discrete games, and the World Series conforms to this basic property of the sport.

We encounter the same phenomenon in other sports as well. For example, we feel no particular sympathy for the tennis player who loses a match 6-7, 6-0, 6-7, even though she won 18 games and her opponent only 14. Whereas the "game" is the paramount unit in baseball, the "set" takes precedence in tennis.

Presidential elections, however, are not a sporting event (in which the rules are inherently arbitrary), but rather an effort to select as chief magistrate the person desired by the populace.[149] There is no compelling reason to organize presidential elections in a way that treats electoral votes as the crucial unit (akin to the game in baseball and set in tennis) and allows someone to win an election while receiving fewer actual votes than their opponent.

In short, the most common argument for abolishing the Electoral College derives from the belief that individual voters are the fundamental unit when it comes to elections: Everyone's vote should count equally and the presidency be determined accordingly. The founders may have had esoteric ideas about republican government, but, the argument goes, the winner of elections should be the candidate who receives the most votes—period.[150] Senator Birch Bayh, who long crusaded for abolition of the Electoral College, put the matter well: "Direct election is the only system that guarantees that every vote will count, that every vote will count the same, and that the candidate with the most votes will win."[151]

As Bayh's statement suggests, Electoral College abolitionists generally want the college replaced by a nationwide popular vote. Recognizing the danger of a large field that splinters the vote, thereby allowing the victor to emerge without widespread support, many advocates of a direct, national vote propose a runoff system akin to what some states employ for statewide or local races. Typically, if no candidate receives 40 percent of the vote, the top two face off in a runoff election.

Below, I shall make a different argument for abolishing the Electoral College, one based not on its undemocratic nature but rather on something rarely remarked—namely, that the Electoral College increases the susceptibility of our elections to fraud. First, though, I shall briefly address the major arguments in favor of retaining the Electoral College.

Supporters of the Electoral College note that it is time-tested. At least we know what we're getting, and it has gotten us through fifty-eight presidential elections spanning well over 200 years. True, in practice the Electoral College bears little resemblance to what the founders envisioned, but, given the law of unintended consequences, we should nevertheless exercise caution about replacing it.[152] Abolish the Electoral College and who knows what problems will arise from its replacement.

This argument, however, sets the bar for success too low. Even if we ignore other problems with the Electoral College, including the five times a president received fewer votes than his or her opponent, it has produced three crises. (I'm exempting the election of 1800, in which the crisis stemmed from a constitutional glitch repaired by the Twelfth Amendment.) This hardly seems a remarkable track record. And, as discussed below, the prospect of an election crisis has increased.

Supporters of the Electoral College also claim that it promotes the constitutionally important principle of "federalism," forcing candidates to consider the interests of states. Professor Akhil Amar, one of America's preeminent constitutional scholars, shrugs off this claim:

In the current system, candidates don't appeal so much to state interests (what are those, anyway?) as to demographic groups (elderly voters, soccer moms) within states. And direct popular elections would still encourage candidates to take into account regional differences, like those between voters in the Midwest and the East. After all, one cannot win a national majority without getting lots of votes in lots of places.[153]

What about the widespread view that the Electoral College protects the interests of *small* states? Since even the tiniest states have three electoral votes, candidates will pay attention to them. Compare the least populous state (Wyoming) to the most (California): Wyoming has 544,000 people, California 39.5 million. Thus California's population is roughly seventy-five times greater than Wyoming's, but California's advantage in electoral votes (55 to 3) is only eighteen times greater. No presidential candidate would bother to campaign in Wyoming were it not for the fact that the Electoral College amplifies its relevance. As it happens, Wyoming is a reliably Republican state, so presidential candidates don't campaign there anyway. But more contested small states, such as Nevada, New Hampshire, and Maine, may attract candidates thanks to their electoral votes.

There are a number of flaws with this argument. For starters, when it comes to where presidential candidates campaign, the Electoral College taketh away more than it giveth. If New Hampshirites and Nevadans benefit, what about Californians, New Yorkers, and Texans? Because these large states are not swing states, they rarely see candidates in the flesh (except, of course, for fundraising events). Is it really a good thing if candidates campaign in sparsely populated states while ignoring states with millions more people?

The assumption that candidates visit small states on account of the Electoral College turns out to be false. In the 2000 election, for example, the twenty least populous states received a combined nine visits from candidates Gore and Bush. By contrast, Georgia alone received eleven. During the final seven months of the campaign, fourteen states received *zero* presidential visits. All fourteen had eight or fewer electoral votes. So much for the Electoral College raising the relevance and visibility of small states.

The effect of the Electoral College on presidential campaigns is not to attract candidates to small states but rather to funnel the candidates to sizable swing states. Thus, in 2000, the candidates made frequent visits to Illinois (eighteen), Pennsylvania (twelve), and Ohio (eleven). The combined visits to those three states alone exceeded the combined visits to the forty least visited states. The same phenomenon occurred during the most recent close election, 2016: Two-thirds of all campaign events were held in just six states (the smallest of which, Virginia, is not small) and 94 percent of events took place in twelve states. To make matters worse, the focus on swing states means that, to a large extent, the same states in election after election see the candidates most, with the vast majority of voters nationwide perpetually ignored. One political scientist who studied the history of presidential campaigns summarized the situation as follows: "Candidates are not fools. They go where the Electoral College makes them go, and it makes them go to competitive states, especially large competitive states. They ignore most small states; in fact, they ignore most of the country."[154]

If we look at candidates' media advertising and mailings, instead of just visits, we see the same thing. Should you happen to live in a swing state, you will (for better and worse) be bombarded by advertisements from the presidential candidates and independent groups that support them. If you don't live in a swing state, you will be ignored. The objective of seeing presidential candidates campaign in more places is hindered, not helped, by the Electoral College.

To be fair, supporters of the Electoral College make the argument about candidate visits as part of a larger argument that the Electoral College promotes the interests of small states. However, the former figures to be a near perfect proxy for the latter. If candidates don't worry about small states enough to campaign there, why would they worry about them when in office? As a historical matter, the notion that the framers envisioned the Electoral College as protecting small states is dubious. In recent years, eminent founding-era historians have shown that creating the Electoral College was less about small states and big states than about free states and slave states —with the anti-slavery North making concessions to the slave-driven South.[155] Consider the constitutional provision counting slaves as three-fifths of a person for the purposes of apportioning representatives. This notorious clause increased the number of electoral votes accorded slave states, and thus enhanced the power of those states. (To this day, some white supremacists see the Electoral College as a means of perpetuating racial dominance in the United States.[156])

Perhaps the lowest moment of the Constitutional Convention came when none other than James Madison, the deservedly anointed father of the Constitution, protested against the idea of a direct, national popular vote to determine the presidency: "The right of suffrage was much more diffusive in the northern than the southern states; and the latter could have no influence on the election on the score of negroes."[157] The uncharacteristically awkward formulation may reflect Madison's moral uneasiness, but his sentiment can be translated as follows: "Of course slaves are just property and can't vote, but we who own this property want to count them as if they were fully human so as to increase our political power." Counting enslaved black people, albeit at a degrading two-fifths discount, perversely empowered the white supremacist South. This cynical racism worked to perfection: "More than one in four U.S. presidents were involved in human trafficking and slavery," observes Clarence Lusane in his aptly titled book *A Black History of the White House*. The prevalence of slave-owning presidents resulted directly from the Electoral College.

For example, as Akhil Amar reminds us, in Thomas Jefferson's victory over John Adams in the election of 1800, "the slavery-skew of the electoral college was the decisive margin of victory: without the extra electoral college votes generated by slavery, the mostly southern states that supported Jefferson would not have sufficed to give him a majority. As pointed observers remarked at the time, Thomas Jefferson metaphorically rode into the executive mansion on the backs of slaves."[158]

A mythology has built up around the Electoral College, the idea that it occupies a special place in the Founding Fathers' intricate constitutional architecture and reflects sophisticated thinking—in contrast to the simpleminded idea of electing the president directly through the popular vote. In fact, quite a few founders, including some of the shrewdest like Gouverneur Morris, supported direct election of the president.[159] It is likely no coincidence that Morris was an anti-slavery Northerner.

Even putting aside the Electoral College's role as an instrument of white supremacy, the notion that the college helps small states rests partly on a confusion. It is certainly true that giving each state two senators, regardless of population, enhances the power of states in general and small states in particular. To take the example noted earlier, Wyoming has one-eighteenth the representation in Congress of California despite having only one seventy-fifth of its population. But the benefits of this arrangement have little to do with the Electoral College. Few who want to abolish the Electoral College have suggested abolishing or changing the composition of the Senate (which cannot be done anyway).[160] Rather, we see little value in this federalist principle when it comes to electing the one person who is directly and solely responsible for the good of the entire nation.[161] Wyoming and other small states have a disproportionate say in the Congress. It is hardly imperative that they also have a disproportionate influence on the executive branch.[162] Consider that no law can pass without the Senate signing on. That alone offers significant protection to small states.

If the alleged advantages of the Electoral College are overrated, its fundamentally undemocratic nature and white supremacist legacy may be reason enough to abolish it. Opponents of the college have tried mightily; members of Congress have introduced more than 1,000 proposed constitutional amendments to alter or abolish the Electoral College. No other clause has attracted close to this many proposed amendments. But these efforts have failed to gain traction. Abolition of the Electoral College apparently requires additional arguments beyond the emphasis on equality and democracy.

Below, I advance a different reason for abolishing the Electoral College, one that has more salience today than ever before. While my argument is informed by the elections of 1824, 1876, and 2000 (and to a lesser extent 2016), my concern is not that the wrong man won in those crisis elections. Rather, my concern is the crises themselves. They proved divisive for the nation and could have turned out worse. Next time we may not be so lucky as to see a peaceful and sufficiently timely resolution. My argument against the Electoral College is that it invites crisis and fraud, a risk that has become greater in the age of hacking.

THE ELECTORAL COLLEGE INVITES CRISIS AND FRAUD

The elections of 1824, 1876, 2000, and 2016 were not particularly close in the national popular vote. Andrew Jackson received 38,000 more votes than John Quincy Adams, a veritable landslide; Jackson received 41 percent of the vote and Adams just 31 percent (with the caveat that in six states' electors were chosen by the state legislature rather than popular vote). Samuel Tilden received 254,000 more votes than Rutherford B. Hayes, a much smaller win in percentage terms, but still a decisive 3 percent. Had the winner of these elections been determined by national popular vote, corrupt bargains and partisan commissions would not have entered the picture. The 2000 election was far closer in percentage terms (0.7 percent), but Al Gore received 544,000 more votes than George W. Bush. Without the Electoral College, there would have been a clear winner and no need for a controversial Supreme Court decision that compromised the legitimacy of both the President and the Court.[163] So too, the popular vote gap in 2016 was almost 3 million.

Curiously, supporters of the Electoral College

sometimes argue that it *increases* the likelihood of a decisive winner. For example, an influential American Enterprise Institute (AEI) essay defending the Electoral College insisted that "the American electorate has a fundamental tendency to finish closely, with 'photo finish' elections. . . . In purely numerical popular votes, an election might be uncertain and vulnerable to challenge; but the Electoral College replaces the numerical uncertainty with an unambiguously visible constitutional majority."[164]

On rare occasion, presidential elections have played out as the AEI envisions. In 1968, Richard Nixon's advantage over Hubert Humphrey was less than 1 percent in the popular vote but a commanding 20 percent in the Electoral College. In the nineteenth century (when there were vastly fewer votes, and thus a far greater likelihood of a national squeaker), this happened several times, most notably in 1880, when James Garfield received just 1,898 more votes than Winifred Hancock yet won handily in the Electoral College. But far more often the opposite has been the case, with elections producing a comfortable popular vote margin accompanied by a thin margin in the Electoral College—thin enough that one or two states going differently would have changed the outcome.[165] Putting aside the election of 1876, but sticking to the nineteenth century, in 1844, 1848, and 1884, the popular vote margin was reasonably decisive (340,000, 1.3 million, and 58,000 respectively) whereas, a switch of 3,300 or fewer votes in one or two states would have produced a different result in the Electoral College.

This happened even more often in the twentieth century, with the 1916 election presenting a perfect example. Woodrow Wilson received 578,000 more votes than Charles Evan Hughes, a fairly comfortable margin. However, he received only 277 electoral votes (to Hughes's 254), and barely won several states. At the national level, it would have taken a switch of 289,000 votes to change the outcome. By contrast, a flip of a mere 1,867 votes in California would have given Hughes the election. Wilson also won New Hampshire's four electoral votes by fifty-six votes(!) and North Dakota's five by 1,735. A switch of just 895 votes in those two states combined would have flipped nine electoral votes from Wilson's column to Hughes's. In other words, a switch of a mere 2,763 votes would have left Hughes with 275 electoral votes and Wilson 256—basically reversing their actual totals. That is less than 1 percent of the number of votes that would have had to flip to make Hughes the winner in the national popular vote.

The 1916 election was far closer to the norm than to the exception. As a straightforward historical fact, the Electoral College produces squeakers far more often than does the national popular vote. In 1948, for example, a flip of just 31,000 votes in four states (Illinois, Ohio, California, Idaho) would have made Thomas Dewey president, despite the fact that Harry Truman won the national vote handily. To change the latter, Dewey would have needed to flip well over 1 million Truman votes to his column. Similarly, in 1976, Gerald Ford would have defeated Jimmy Carter with a shift of just over 9,000 votes combined in Ohio and Hawaii. A shift of an additional 7,000 in Mississippi and Ford would have won the Electoral College with room to spare. For Ford to have won the national popular vote, however, would have required flipping 841,000 votes. Overall, we have experienced twenty-two "hair's-breadth elections" in the Electoral College, most of which produced substantial popular vote margins.[166]

As noted, the 2016 election provides another excellent example. Hillary Clinton received 2.87 million more votes than Donald Trump. By contrast, a swing of fewer than 62,000 votes in Florida and Michigan combined would have changed the Electoral College from Trump to Clinton. Tiny swings in Pennsylvania and Wisconsin, and small swings in Arizona and North Carolina, would have changed the Electoral College result dramatically. Similarly, in 2000, Florida was not the only state in which a small switch of votes would have changed the Electoral College outcome. George W. Bush won four other states (Missouri, Nevada, Tennessee, and New Hampshire), totaling thirty-nine electoral votes, by minuscule margins. With a swing of fewer than 100,000 votes in these states combined, Al Gore would have won the Electoral College comfortably instead of losing it. Again, that's not even counting Florida's twenty-five electoral votes.[167] By contrast, 272,000 Gore votes would have to have swung to Bush to change the popular vote winner.

In both 2000 and 2016, the Electoral College presented hackers and other perpetrators of fraud with golden opportunities. In each case, they would have had to tamper with a small number of ballots in a few states to produce a different outcome—exponentially fewer than the number of ballots they would have had to tamper with to affect the outcome in the national popular vote. This has been true in no fewer than nine presidential elections, whereas the reverse (a virtual tie in the national popular vote) has occurred just once: the aforementioned 1880 election.

As noted above, the opposite is sometimes suggested—that the Electoral College *reduces* the risk of fraud and endless recounts. Theoretically, this claim makes sense, because the Electoral College renders the exact tally in each state irrelevant unless it is extremely close. But historically, the idea that the Electoral College magnifies the winner's margin has been debunked.[168] On the contrary, the Electoral College enhances the risk of a close race whose outcome can be affected through relatively modest—and therefore more difficult to detect—manipulation. Indeed, while not referencing the Electoral College specifically, a cybersecurity think tank made this key point in the ominously-titled book, *Hacking Elections Is Easy*: "By focusing on the machines in swing regions of swing states, an election can be hacked without drawing considerable notice."[169]

It may be countered that, while it is technically true

that hackers and other election fraudsters can more easily sabotage the Electoral College because they would need to change relatively few votes, this advantage is illusory, because the would-be infiltrators cannot know in advance which states will be razor close.[170] But such a claim is empirically shaky. In this era of advanced analytics and polling, everyone pretty much knows which handful of states realistically could go to either candidate.

A potentially stronger objection to the argument that hackers would have an easier time dictating the outcome in the Electoral College is that the data supporting this conclusion might have been different if the winner of prior elections had been determined by the national popular vote. After all, candidates have designed their campaigns with the Electoral College in mind, and would campaign differently if the result were determined differently. And if the candidates campaigned differently, the results might differ too. We cannot assume that we would end up with the fairly comfortable national margin that has been the norm.

It is certainly true that, if a national popular vote determined the winner, candidates would campaign differently—for example, paying more attention to heavily populated non-swing states and less to smaller swing states. However, there is no reason to believe that the different campaign strategies dictated by a system that measured only the popular vote would significantly affect the overall margin of that vote nationwide.

Consider, as a thought experiment, the 2000 presidential election, focusing on California and New Hampshire—exactly the kind of states that would presumably be treated differently by the candidates if the Electoral College were replaced by a national popular vote. George W. Bush won New Hampshire's four electoral votes by fewer than 7,200 votes out of just 540,000 cast, whereas Al Gore won California's fifty-five electoral votes by more than 1.2 million out of roughly 10.4 million cast. Had the winner of the election been determined by national popular vote, surely the candidates would have focused substantial attention on California and little on New Hampshire. (Put aside the fact, discussed above, that even under the status quo general election candidates pay little attention to small states like New Hampshire.) But would this have substantially affected the outcome in either state? Probably not, because *both* candidates would have changed their behavior with respect to these states. Is there good reason to believe that California would have been less lopsided had both candidates (instead of neither) campaigned there extensively?

To be sure, we can posit reasons why the vote count might have been significantly different. Maybe, for example, one of the candidates held more effective rallies. Maybe more people would have voted, and most of the new voters would have favored one candidate. Today, people living in decisively red or blue states may think their vote a waste. Some evidence suggests that people favoring the losing candidate are more likely to stay home if the election is perceived as one-sided. If true, replacing the Electoral College with a national popular vote would encourage Democrats in Texas and Republicans in California and New York to come out and vote.[171] Conceivably that would make the national margin closer, though there is no particular reason to assume that. And, of course, encouraging more voters can be seen as a good thing and therefore another argument against the Electoral College.

Given the law of unintended consequences, it is always possible that moving to a national popular vote would backfire and make presidential elections more rather than less prone to crisis and fraud. However, we must act on the best information available, and failing to act is a form of action. Extensive historical evidence indicates that the Electoral College increases our susceptibility to squeakers and therefore to crisis and fraud. Especially in the age of hacking, it is irresponsible not to consider this important circumstance when weighing the pros and cons of moving to a direct national election.

Finally, the argument that the Electoral College will produce more squeakers than the national vote does not rest solely on history. It also rests on the basic statistical principle that the greater the sample size, the greater the variation.[172] Imagine there were only ten voters in every state. Assuming the candidates are equal, as a sheer matter of probability the fifty states would be almost certain to produce many five-five ties. By contrast, it is extremely unlikely that the overall national tally of the 500 votes will produce a 250-250 tie. When we map this insight onto the 2000 election, we realize that it makes good sense, probabilistically, that several states were exceptionally close, whereas the margin separating the candidates nationally exceeded 500,000 votes.[173] The national *percentage* difference was small (though still vastly greater than that in Florida), but would-be hackers aren't concerned with percentages. As noted, they would have had to flip 272,000 votes to affect the national vote winner and only a few hundred to affect the winner in Florida—and therefore the Electoral College.

In the wake of the 2000 election, eminent historian Jack Rakove asked, rhetorically, "How do the Republic and the Union benefit when an election can turn on a flawed ballot design in a single county or a single state?"[174] This sensible question needs to be broadened: How do we benefit when the election can turn on a single hack or other act of fraud in a single county or a single state?

It may be countered that, if the national popular vote is close, the result could produce chaos far greater than occurred even in 2000, when at least the mayhem was localized in one state. As Judge Richard Posner says, "A national recount would be an expensive nightmare."[175] Posner maintains that, had the Bush-Gore race been determined by popular vote, "there is little doubt that if Bush's people nosed around heavily Democratic precincts throughout the nation they would come up with colorable arguments about voter and tabulation errors . . . that might have made the difference" and thus justified a recount.[176] In large part for this reason, Posner concludes that abolishing the Electoral College "would exacerbate the problem of disputed Presidential elections."[177]

But note that Posner concedes that Bush winning a recount "would have been a long shot, given Gore's popular-vote margin."[178] Such a long shot, one might say, that a recount would have made little sense. As noted, there has been only one presidential election (1880) in which the national popular vote produced such a squeaker that a recount would rationally be deemed useful. The answer to Posner's argument, then, is that the national popular vote exacerbates disputed presidential elections only if there is a legitimate dispute—and, the evidence suggests, there rarely will be.[179]

Of course, as Posner indicates, the losing candidate may wish to toss a Hail Mary. The solution to this problem is to come up with a rational scheme for dealing with election disputes, which includes a mechanism for determining when a recount is worth undertaking. Posner means to evoke the behavior of the candidates in 2000, "nosing around" and making "colorable arguments," but that fiasco took place in a state with a convoluted election code that encouraged scheming and had no clear means of adjudicating disputes. In the next chapter, I will propose a nationwide mechanism for reducing such chaos. Indeed, I package it with my call for abolition of the Electoral College into a single proposed constitutional amendment.[180]

Everything is a case of *compared to what*? Perhaps the Electoral College is, as Churchill said of democracy, the worst system except for all the others. We should at least briefly touch on the major alleged flaw with a direct national vote: It would weaken the two-party system. Today, the argument goes, third parties typically have little impact on presidential elections because they rarely acquire electoral votes. If we abolished the Electoral College, third parties would be empowered by their popular vote totals. Suppose that the new election law provides for a runoff between the top two finishers if no candidate receives 40 percent of the vote. (As noted, many Electoral College abolitionists favor such a provision.) Third-party candidates could prevent any candidate from receiving 40 percent and then hold major cards for the runoff, offering their public support in exchange for some role or influence in the next administration.

However, such minor-party mischief is equally possible within the Electoral College system. If a third-party candidate threatens to take a sufficient number of votes from another candidate in a few states, he or she may have enormous leverage. Many argue that Ralph Nader cost Al Gore the presidency in 2000, a foreseeable result. (Nor was this a fluky outcome. Though the data are inconclusive, many people believe that Ross Perot cost George Bush the 1992 election.) Had he been so inclined, Nader could have sought to extract promises from Gore in exchange for dropping out of the race. It makes little difference whether such bargaining takes place before Election Day or after the initial election but prior to the runoff.

Note that all fifty states elect governors without the

benefit of an electoral college. There is no evidence that such races are generally marred or disproportionately influenced by third-party candidates. Occasionally a viable third-party candidate produces a splintered vote or otherwise significantly influences the race. Occasionally that happens in presidential elections too, despite the Electoral College.

Anyone who finds the arguments in this chapter unpersuasive, and remains attached to the Electoral College, should at least consider a compromise that would retain the Electoral College but greatly reduce the extent to which it invites fraud and crisis. Having fifty-one separate elections (the District of Columbia along with the states), the tampering with any of which can dictate the overall winner, increases the risk of fraud and crisis mainly because forty-nine of those fifty-one elections determine electoral votes on a winner-take-all basis. If we keep the Electoral College, but allocate candidates' electoral votes proportionally to their statewide popular vote, the risk of outcome-determinative tampering will plummet.

George W. Bush and Al Gore almost perfectly split Florida's 6 million votes. Does it make sense that one of them received twenty-five electoral votes and the other zero? This wildly lopsided allocation seems unfair to the losing candidate of a close state (and his or her voters) and difficult to justify.[181] More importantly, for present purposes, apportioning votes would disincentivize fraud. Consider that, in 2000, flipping a few hundred votes in Florida would have meant a swing of fifty electoral votes.

If proportional voting were used instead of the "unit" rule (so-called because each state's votes are treated as a single unit), flipping those same few hundred votes would mean a flip of just two electoral votes.[182] Professor Robert Bennett rightly observes that the winner-take-all system "magnifies the significance of what otherwise might be relatively trivial disputes."[183]

Defenders of the unit rule will counter that, under proportional allocations, Ralph Nader and Pat Buchanan would have picked up electoral votes in Florida and elsewhere—reducing the bottom-line vote of the winner and encouraging new parties, thereby weakening the two-party system. To avoid that result, however, we need only stipulate that electoral votes are allocated to the top two finishers in the state, according to their percentage of the vote relative to one another. Alternatively, we could provide that candidates must receive at least 10 percent of the vote in a given state to qualify for electoral votes. Third-party candidates rarely reach that threshold. Nader and Buchanan failed to reach that threshold in a single state.[184]

Replacing the unit rule with proportional allocation would likely have a collateral benefit: encouraging people to vote. As noted, under the unit rule, voters in many states consider their vote a waste because the outcome in their state is a foregone conclusion.[185] Under proportional allocation, their votes would be every bit as meaningful as that of voters in swing states. And, it should be added, the winner-take-all approach was not mandated by the

Constitution nor expected by the Founding Fathers. It emerged as a kind of race to the bottom, in which the kingmakers who controlled state delegations wished to maximize their own power, forcing their counterparts in other states to follow suit. The unit rule served parochial interests, not the national interest.[186]

A possible negative result of proportional allocation would be the occasional election thrown into the House of Representatives. In 1992, for example, Ross Perot's 19 percent of the vote would have translated to a fair number of electoral votes, likely denying Bill Clinton a majority. Once again, this risk can be eliminated if electoral votes are apportioned only between the top two vote-getters. Moreover, the risk of an election thrown to the House can occur under the winner-take-all status quo as well, and is more likely to do so with a candidate who has purely regional appeal, such as George Wallace. In 1968, Wallace received forty-six electoral votes, and came reasonably close to throwing the election to the House. The fact that Wallace's 13.5 percent of the vote translated to forty-six more electoral votes than those received by Perot, who garnered millions more votes, is itself a data point suggesting flaws in the winner-take-all system. (Or, for a more apples-to-apples comparison, in 1948 Henry Wallace received just 13,000 fewer votes than Strom Thurmond but came away with zero electoral votes to Thurmond's thirty-nine.) Indeed, in the 1992 election, Bill Clinton received just 46 percent of the vote in California but 100 percent of its electoral votes—a whopping fifty-four, a full 20 percent of the requisite 270 to make him president. This distortion is problematic.

To scrap the winner-take-all allocation of electoral votes in favor of proportional allocation while preserving the Electoral College would not require a constitutional amendment. States already have the authority, under Article II, to determine how electors are chosen. However, some states will be reluctant to allocate electoral votes proportionally if other states remain winner-take-all. For one thing, the leaders of a reliably red state like Texas would hardly consent to an approach that would give the Democratic candidate a substantial number of electors if their counterparts in blue states like California did not do the same. In addition, candidates would arguably be incentivized to pay more attention to the winner-take-all states (at least the swing states among them), where they would get more bang for their campaign buck because a narrow victory or defeat would have greater electoral consequences. For both of these reasons, while individual states have the authority to adopt proportional allocation on their own, realistically a constitutional amendment may be needed.

As it happens, it may be possible to *abolish* the Electoral College (effectively) without amending the Constitution. Three constitutional scholars, Akhil Amar, Vikram Amar, and Robert Bennett, arrived at the counterintuitive conclusion that we can effectively eliminate the Electoral College without amending the Constitution.[187] All it takes is for a bunch of states (totaling 270 or more electoral votes) to require their electors to cast their votes for the candidate who receives the most votes nationwide.

Beginning in 2006, states began putting into action the approach advocated by the Amars and Bennett, approving what they call the National Popular Vote Interstate Compact (NPVIC). This compact entails states agreeing to have their electors support whichever candidate receives the most votes nationwide, provided enough other states agree to do the same. As long as the states entering this compact comprise 270 or more electoral votes, we will be assured that the winner of the national popular vote becomes president. In early 2019, Colorado became the fourteenth jurisdiction (thirteen states plus the District of Columbia) to enact the NPVIC. Those states combine for 181 electoral votes, leaving the compact just eighty-nine votes short of effectively converting U.S. presidential elections into a nationwide popular vote.

For the most part, support and opposition to NPVIC simply tracks the debate for and against the Electoral College.[188] However, opponents of the NPVIC also make an argument specific to the NPVIC: It is unconstitutional. Certainly, on its face, NPVIC seems like an end-run around the Constitution, which establishes the Electoral College as the means of selecting a president.

This argument is unconvincing. As noted, the Constitution authorizes each state to determine how its electors will be selected. The NPVIC would simply provide a new method of selection—choosing electors who will do the nation's bidding (as determined by state law). Some opponents of the NPVIC argue that states cannot bind electors to vote a certain way. However, it is already the case that more than half the states bind electors to vote for the winner of their state. Thus legislating against the "faithless elector" already occurs: The NPVIC would simply bind the electors to a different outcome—to vote for the winner of the nation's popular vote rather than the state's.

Some opponents claim that the NPVIC violates the Constitution's provision (in Article I, Section 10, Clause 3) that "No state shall, without the consent of Congress . . . enter into any agreement or compact with another state." However, whether the NPVIC even constitutes an interstate compact, at least of the sort contemplated by the Constitution, is an open question.[189] Even if the NPVIC is deemed an interstate compact for Article 1 purposes, at most that would mean that the NPVIC requires congressional endorsement.[190]

There are, to be sure, other possible objections to NPVIC, including the practical concern that it does not (and cannot) require a runoff between the top two national vote-getters. By effectively abolishing the Electoral College without requiring such a runoff, the NPVIC could increase the risk of a low-plurality president in a multicandidate field. There are many ways of addressing this problem, whose scope lies beyond this book.[191]

Another potential problem with the NPVIC is that it might not achieve the main goal of Electoral College abolitionists—ensuring equal voting power for all citizens. True, if the NPVIC won out, the votes of citizens in all states would count the same. Some people, however, would not be able to vote at all because of the eligibility requirements in their state. Of course, that is the system we have now. For example, some states permit seventeen-year-olds to vote, whereas others do not; some states make it easier than others to vote early or by absentee ballot. But the numerous differences in state laws' treatment of prospective voters in the presidential election are considered acceptable in a system in which the presidential election basically involves fifty-one separate elections, the results of which are aggregated in the Electoral College. By contrast, a national popular vote would place all votes in a single pool and supposedly treat all citizens equally. It will fail to do so, however, as long as states have different rules governing voting procedures and eligibility.

Accordingly, the move to achieve a national popular vote, whether by constitutional amendment, interstate compact, or any other means, would ideally be accompanied by the establishment of uniform rules governing presidential elections.[192]

SEVEN

A CONSTITUTIONAL AMENDMENT FOR HANDLING FUTURE CRISES

Abolition of the Electoral College would reduce but not eliminate the dangers of a presidential election marred by fraud and post-election chaos. We obviously cannot rule out a national popular vote producing a virtual tie amidst credible allegations of covert manipulation, hacking, or voter-tabulation problems that call into question the accuracy of the count. A major lesson to be learned from the elections of 1876 and 2000 is that we lack a mechanism for reliably resolving such disputes in a way that preserves legitimacy and gives all sides a reasonable degree of confidence in at least the process, if not necessarily the outcome.

The experience of Florida in 2000 also reminds us that numerous things can go wrong. While Florida's flawed election law produced some of these problems, not even the clearest and most thorough election code can assure that a disputed election will be resolved in a timely and reliable fashion. No legislature, state or federal, can possibly anticipate all of the problems that may arise in an election. Even when problems *can* be anticipated, their exact nature may remain unknown, preventing them from being easily redressed. Consider malfunctioning equipment, inclement weather, and other logistical problems that cause certain precincts to be shut down for a period of time on Election Day. This is something we know will happen, yet it nevertheless presents judgment calls that will vary from case to case. May (must?) the polls be kept open longer in these precincts? How much longer? Presumably that depends on the cause and severity of the problem. What happens if a hurricane or other natural disaster prevents voting for the entire day in certain locations? If even this foreseeable problem does not lend itself to a perfectly satisfactory solution, imagine the havoc wreaked by the many potential problems that cannot be foreseen.

In part for that reason, abolishing the Electoral College will not guarantee the end of presidential election crises, especially now that hackers in multiple countries are working to infiltrate our voting systems. It is, therefore, imperative that we find a better means for dealing with the kinds of scenarios that arose in 1876 and 2000. To some extent, this has been recognized. Following the 2000 debacle, the Carter-Ford commission was hardly the only effort to explore how to prevent future election crises. Any number of books have been written and legal symposia organized around this very question: How do we prevent another 2000?

Unfortunately, reformers thought too locally. For example, the Help America Vote Act (HAVA) abolished punch-card ballots and requires provisional ballots. But punch-card ballots and voters turned away were only two among many issues in Florida in 2000; Florida was just one state and 2000 was just one election. HAVA's helpful steps barely begin to guard against future crises. States adopted assorted reforms, many of them clarifying rules governing elections, such as the procedures for voter registration, absentee ballots, and improved voting technologies. These welcome developments, too, failed to address a central issue: How do we respond to another 1876 or 2000? Even if the mechanics of casting and counting ballots were perfected, elections would still be prone to fraud by hackers and others. While doing everything possible to make sure elections unfold properly, we must also position ourselves to handle scenarios in which they do not.[193]

Such efforts are more necessary than ever. We used to worry about conventional fraud by U.S. citizens. In some precincts in Chicago, for example, people, including the deceased, seemed capable of casting multiple ballots. Such chicanery hasn't disappeared, but the advent of hacking has multiplied the risk of election fraud. It has also multiplied the risk of chicanery that takes longer to detect, something that must be taken into account when we fashion measures for responding to election crises.

While our government should work to develop an impenetrable voting infrastructure system, we need to be realistic, and the history of election technology does not inspire confidence.[194] Who would have thought that butterfly ballots and hanging chads would become decisive features in a twenty-first-century presidential election? While we need to aim for the best, we must prepare for the worst—meaning we must develop a fallback plan in case there is reason to believe that voting systems were hacked (or if, due to another form of fraud or for any reason, the outcome of an election is uncertain).

When we scrutinize past crisis elections, we see three fundamental problems: time pressure, the ad hoc nature of resolving disputes, and partisanship.

The attempt to determine the actual winner was undertaken under serious time pressure. Regrettably, this problem was actually far greater in 2000 than in 1876. In 1876, the nation had until March 4 to determine the winner. That had been the presidential inauguration date beginning with George Washington's second term, though it was not stipulated by the Constitution. The Twentieth Amendment, ratified in 1933, changed the date to January 20. That change, made to hasten the transition from one president to the next and to reduce the period with a lame duck president, produced an unintended consequence: It left little time to resolve uncertainty over the winner of the election.

With inauguration required by January 20, Congress established January 6 as the day its joint session of Congress counts and records the Electoral College's votes. The electors meet to cast those votes on the first Monday after the second weekend in December, which in 2000 was December 18. The safe harbor date (guaranteeing that a state's electoral votes will be accepted) is six days before the Electoral College meets, meaning that in 2000 it fell on December 12—a little more than a month after Election Day. On account of this compressed time frame, the attempt to handle the murky post-election situation in Florida occurred at warp speed. The United States Supreme Court's dubious determination that Florida law incorporates the safe harbor led the Court to stop the recount on December 12. Justice Stevens opined that Florida had until January 6 to select its electors, whereas Justice Souter and many commentators would have split that difference and given Florida until December 18.[195] For present purposes, what matters is that January 6, the last possible date, was still all too soon.

The resulting problem was twofold. First, while six justices believed that a statewide recount in Florida was called for, only four justices thought there was adequate time. Accordingly, Florida's effort to determine the statewide (and thus national) winner was deemed doomed for lack of time. Second, everyone involved in the process—the canvassing boards, various state officials including the secretary of state, and the assorted state and federal judges to hear aspects of the case—was forced into hasty action. Fast cases make bad law and bad policy.

A few examples will suffice. As noted, Al Gore's

lawyers requested a recount in four heavily Democratic precincts only, a move that may have cost Gore dearly (by leaving much less time for the statewide recount eventually ordered by the Florida Supreme Court). Asked about that decision, Dexter Douglas, a prominent Florida lawyer who served on Gore's legal team, explained, "I'm not sure that we ever really had a chance to consider this, we didn't figure we had time to do [a statewide recount]."[196] Note the double whammy here—Gore's lawyers lacked time to consider the issue, but to the extent they did consider asking for a statewide recount, they concluded that there was insufficient time. Time after time (so to speak), haste made waste for Gore's team. Why didn't they ask a Florida court to establish a statewide standard for the recounts, thereby avoiding the equal protection issue that proved fatal? Douglas claims that he proposed making such a request, but that Gore's lead lawyer, David Boise, responded, "We don't have time, the judge [Terry Lewis] has his hands full."[197]

This might be thought sour grapes by the side that lost, were it not for the fact that Bush's legal team concurs. Barry Richards, a key member of that team, compared the Florida litigation to a "high-speed sailboat race in the high seas in the middle of the storm. . . . So we were making snap decisions as best we could with very little to go on."[198]

It may be that none of this mattered, as perhaps the U.S. Supreme Court was determined to prevent a statewide recount and would have found a way no matter what.

But it did not help matters that the Gore team's counter-productive tactical decisions were dictated less by the law than by the ticking clock. Because the inauguration date of January 20 is established by the Constitution, without an amendment little can be done to expand the post-election pre-inauguration period and reduce the time pressure. Congress can push back the meeting date for the Electoral College (assuming the college is not abolished) and the date Congress accepts the certification of electors, but the actual vote count must be completed by January 20 at the very latest. Realistically, the winner should be determined at least a few days in advance, allowing a little preparation for the inauguration and transition.

A combination of judicial and legislative action could push all the dates back a few weeks, except for the January 20 inauguration. If the dates were pushed back, the next time a Florida-type situation arises, the courts and others won't be quite as rushed. But a few weeks may not be enough. Accordingly, we need to rethink the January 20 inauguration date. While we've become accustomed to January 20, and there were good reasons for moving the date from March to January, we could and probably should amend the Constitution to make it possible for the date to be postponed under extraordinary circumstances. Below I discuss under what circumstances and by whom that determination would be made. For present purposes, we must take notice that lack of time was a big problem in 1876 and even more so in 2000, and likely will be again, unless we take action.

A second problem with the dispute mechanism process in both 1876 and 2000 was its ad hoc nature. In each case, the state and federal governments lacked a clear pre-existing system designed for such occasions. In 1876, an ad hoc commission was created to determine the winner of the election. In 2000, for better and worse, no such commission was created. No one knew for sure where to turn. Depending on which expert you believed, the correct venue for resolving the election was the Florida courts, the federal courts, the Florida legislature, or the United State Congress. The uncertainty contributed to the thirty-six days of chaos, culminating in the deeply controversial Supreme Court decision.

The most significant problem in both 1876 and 2000 was that the resolution seemed a function of partisanship rather than neutral principles of law, and was accordingly never accepted by the losing party. While commentators on the 2000 election focus on the outcome-determinative decision by the U.S. Supreme Court, we should not ignore the partisanship of the various state officials whose involvement preceded the Court's. Virtually Florida's entire governmental machinery consisted of Republicans with direct or indirect ties to the Bush campaign. That the governor of the state was the brother of the Republican candidate symbolized the problem; the fact that he recused himself from the recount fight in no way eliminated it. Time and again, Secretary of State Harris (who, after all, had been co-chair of Bush's campaign in Florida) and other Republican officials seemed more interested in carrying water for the Republican candidate than in carrying out their duties impartially.[199] Conversely, the Florida Supreme Court consisted primarily of Democrats and ruled consistently for the Democratic candidate. The partisanship of 2000 echoed that of 1876. The commission that made Rutherford B. Hayes president was composed of eight Republicans and seven Democrats, and marked by 8-7 party-line votes favoring the Republican, Hayes. Government officials in all the disputed states also acted in a matter coinciding perfectly with their political affiliations.

These three problems—lack of time, an ad hoc approach, and partisanship—are interrelated, as the 1876 election demonstrates. Lacking a preexisting mechanism for resolving the election dispute, Congress created an ad hoc commission, but Illinois thwarted the plan by selecting Judge David Davis, expected to be the fifteenth (and one impartial) member of the commission, to the U.S. Senate. Davis's replacement, like the other fourteen members of the commission, voted along party lines. Despite a genuine effort by Congress to seek a nonpartisan solution, the time pressure and absence of a preexisting commission led to a partisan outcome.

When we focus on the three problems that plagued the 1876 and 2000 elections, the nature of a solution should be clear: a preexisting nonpartisan commission empowered to resolve disputed presidential elections and given ample time to do so.

A PRESIDENTIAL ELECTION REVIEW BOARD

The solution to a disputed presidential election is a *permanent* nonpartisan commission.[200] The commission could be created by statute, but, as noted, a constitutional amendment would be required to make the January 20 inauguration flexible—that is, to allow the commission to postpone it under certain conditions. But we're getting ahead of ourselves. Before discussing the commission's powers, we must address preliminary matters about the nature of the necessary tribunal.

History provides useful guidance. We can start by learning from the failure of the commission created during the 1876 imbroglio. As noted, that commission's failure can be traced to its composition: The commission included more Republicans than Democrats, and almost every determination it made broke down along partisan lines. Members of Congress anticipated this risk, and sought a commission with an equal number of Democrats and Republicans along with the nonpartisan Justice Davis. While their laudable goal was thwarted, the lesson is clear: What I will call the Presidential Election Review Board (PERB) must have an equal number of Democrats and Republicans. As discussed shortly, it should not consist only of Democrats and Republicans.

History also provides an example of a more successful means of resolving a disputed election, one that was used by Minnesota on two occasions: the 1962 gubernatorial race and 2008 U.S. Senate race. A brief review of that history will illuminate how we should prepare for future election crises.[201]

Minnesota's Success Stories

The 1962 election between the Republican incumbent, Elmer Andersen, and his Democratic opponent, Karl Rolvaag, was so tight that the winner was not determined until mid-March, more than four months after voters cast their ballots. From November 6 (Election Day) until November 20 (the statutory day for certification), the lead seesawed as precincts around the state issued revised counts. On November 20, Anderson led by a few votes, but the State Canvassing Board declined to certify him the winner, because precincts continued to adjust their tallies. On November 26, the five-member board announced that it could not reach a decision. Two Democrats claimed Rolvaag had won, two Republicans favored Anderson, and the fifth board member, a Republican, abstained, claiming that only the State Supreme Court could make the call. The case soon ended up there, and produced a three-two decision (with two Justices recusing themselves because they served on the board), also along party lines, making Anderson the temporary winner.

The loser retained a statutory right to "contest" the election result in trial court. But which court? With the encouragement of the chief justice of the Minnesota Supreme Court, lawyers for the two candidates agreed on a three-judge panel—one judge who had been appointed by a Democrat, one by a Republican, and one who had been appointed to the trial court by a Democrat and the court of appeals by a Republican.

Rolvaag, the one contesting the election, asked for and was granted a statewide recount. Such a recount occurred under the auspices of one hundred recount teams consisting of three members each—a Democrat, a Republican, and a neutral member agreed to by each candidate. The three-judge panel resolved disagreements over particular ballots. The recount, completed on February 5, put Rolvaag back in the lead by 138 votes, but produced 97,000 challenged ballots. The candidates agreed to submit those ballots to ten two-person teams (one Democrat, one Republican) prior to sending them to the three-judge panel if necessary. The bipartisan pairs resolved virtually all of the disputes, leaving only 1,192 ballots for the three-judge panel.

The panel reviewed those ballots and also considered a range of legal claims by the candidates, such as challenges to absentee ballots that did not conform to the statutory standard and challenges to the votes in precincts where alleged administrative failures may have produced tampering. On March 15, the three-judge panel announced that Rolvaag had won by ninety-one votes (out of 1.25 million cast, an insanely thin margin of .0073 percent). The panel claimed that all of its decisions were unanimous. On March 22, Anderson announced that he would not appeal the panel's determination to the Minnesota Supreme Court. Rolvaag became governor.

Especially when compared to the disputed presiden-

tial elections of 1876 and 2000, the 1962 Minnesota gubernatorial race was a staggering success story: There was
never a threat of chaos, and the losing party accepted the
result. As the *Washington Post* put it in an editorial, "the
state of Minnesota has occasion to congratulate itself," as
its resolution of this ridiculously close election "is a trib-
ute to their political stability and maturity, and to their
faith in democratic government."[202]

This successful experience in 1962 proved an invaluable precedent when, almost a half century later,
Minnesota experienced another "tie" election, in the
2008 race for a U.S. Senate seat between incumbent
Democrat-turned-Republican Norm Coleman and
comedian-turned-politician, Democrat Al Franken. On
November 5, the morning after the vote, the Associated
Press called the election for Coleman, because he led by
762 votes with only a handful of small precincts uncounted.
Coleman declared victory; Franken told reporters he expected a recount. Franken noted that this would be the first
recount in Minnesota since 1962, "when I was eleven years
old. I remember that year very clearly for two reasons. The
recount between Elmer L. Anderson and Karl Rolvaag.
And the Gophers were in the Rose Bowl that year."[203] His
recollection indicates that the Anderson-Rolvaag election
made a deep impression on Minnesotans.

The next two weeks witnessed a public relations
battle between the sides about recounts, while precincts
continued to adjust the original count. On November
18, the State Canvassing Board (consisting of two state

Supreme Court justices, two trial judges, and the secretary of state) met for the first time and heard from the campaigns. The next day the board certified Coleman the winner by 215 votes (out of almost 3 million cast, a margin of less than one-hundredth of a point). Since the margin was less than half a percent, Minnesota law required a recount. Because 10 percent of the vote (almost 294,000 ballots) had been by absentee ballot, and many absentees were rejected, Franken's team thought they had a legitimate chance of prevailing.

As in 1962, during the recount process the candidates challenged individual ballots, but far fewer—originally 6,689, whittled down (by the candidates' lawyers withdrawing weak challenges) to just 1,337 sent to the State Canvassing Board. The five-member board reviewed each of these in a process broadcast over the internet. The board, which included two Democrats, two Republicans, and one independent, reached consensus on every ballot. However, state law empowered the board to look only at ballots counted in the original vote, not those disqualified. The latter included a few thousand absentee ballots, and Franken publicly called for inspection of those. (Minnesota election law imposed fairly rigid requirements for absentee votes, but some absentees had been rejected for no apparent reason.) While claiming that it lacked the power to inspect disqualified ballots, the board pointedly called these ballots "uncounted," rather than "rejected," and a few days later the secretary of state instructed local boards to identify and create a pile of wrongly rejected ballots.

On December 5, the day the recounts were supposed to be completed, Coleman still led by 192 votes, at least according to the secretary of state's office—amidst rumors of "missing votes" in mysterious envelopes. Coleman petitioned the Minnesota Supreme Court to declare that uncounted ballots could not be considered. In a weird case of history repeating itself, just as in 1962, two justices recused themselves because they were members of the State Canvassing Board, and on December 18 the remaining five produced a three-two decision along party lines. The Court ruled for Coleman, but with a twist. It agreed with Coleman that votes originally not counted could not be subject to the recount. However, the Court made an exception for ballots that the two candidates and the local election board agreed were wrongly rejected. The Court instructed the candidates' attorneys to examine ballots *in good faith*.

That wasn't good enough for Justice Alan Page, the former star lineman for the Minnesota Vikings of the NFL, whose blistering dissent attacked the "perverse result" in which the Court "has abdicated its role as the defender of the fundamental right to vote."[204] The names had changed, but this was *Bush v. Gore* all over again, with Page playing the role of Justice Stevens, lamenting that a biased decision not to count votes compromised the integrity of the judiciary and democracy. But Stevens's lament came at the very end of the case; Page's disgust with his colleagues proved premature.

By the time the Minnesota Supreme Court decision

was handed down, the ongoing recounts had given Franken a forty-nine-vote lead. Suddenly, the two sides changed their positions on the uncounted ballots: Coleman now wanted them counted and Franken did not. Perhaps more surprisingly, their respective attorneys agreed about most of the ballots identified by the local boards as wrongly rejected. The inclusion of these votes expanded Franken's lead to 225, and on January 5, 2009, the State Canvassing Board announced that he had won. Franken declared victory; Coleman filed an election "contest" which, under Minnesota law, entitled him to a full-blown trial. Meanwhile Franken brought suit in the Minnesota Supreme Court, urging the Court to compel the governor and secretary of state to certify his election in the interim, so that Minnesota would not be without a second senator before the trial was completed. The Court unanimously declined the invitation.

By law, the election contest trial had to commence twenty days after the filing of the contest—January 26. Minnesota law required the chief justice of the Supreme Court to appoint a three-judge panel of district court judges to hear the case. This law was adopted after the 1962 election in order to make permanent the successful approach to that case, but with some tweaking. In 1962, the chief justice urged the parties to agree on a neutral judge, and their attorneys came up with the idea of a three-judge panel and picked the judges themselves. In 2008, the law required the appointment of such a panel, and authorized the chief justice to select it. However, the chief justice was one of the two justices who had recused himself when the case came before the Court earlier, and he decided to remain on the sidelines. The appointing authority fell to the next most senior justice, Alan Page. Page picked the three judges—one of whom had been appointed by a Republican governor, one by a Democrat, and one by an independent, former governor Jesse Ventura.

At the trial, Coleman's lawyers called for the inspection of roughly 5,000 absentee ballots that had been rejected. The court unanimously rejected the request, ruling that it would inspect an uncounted ballot only if Coleman produced evidence that the ballot complied with Minnesota's rigid requirements for absentees. When ballots (submitted by both candidates) fitting that description were produced, and evaluated by the panel, they actually extended Franken's lead to 312.

All things considered, the three-judge panel worked remarkably well, reaching unanimity on virtually all ballots and other decisions. On April 13, more than five months after voters had gone to the polls, the Court issued its final order, accompanied by a sixty-eight-page opinion. Franken remained the winner. Coleman appealed the decision to the Minnesota Supreme Court. On June 30, the Court unanimously affirmed the decision of the three-judge panel. Coleman conceded, and Franken finally assumed office.

There were some complaints in Republican circles. Ben Ginsburg, an election law titan who helped Bush prevail in the 2000 recount and assisted Coleman during the contest trial, was particularly acerbic. He dubbed one key anti-Coleman ruling, handed down by the three-judge panel on Friday, February 13, the "Friday the thirteenth ruling," implying that it belonged in a horror film, and called another ruling by the panel "unprincipled."[205] When the dust settled a few months later, the *Wall Street Journal* editorialized that Franken had "effectively stolen an election."[206]

But these protests came from outside the state. Coleman himself never claimed unfair treatment, and the major Minnesota newspapers that had endorsed him now praised the process that had produced his defeat. The *Minnesota Star Tribune* editorialized that even critics of the time-consuming post-election process "have to admire the result: a clear decision, arrived at with thoroughness and care, and with no evidence of fraud. That makes it possible it will be accepted by people of all political persuasions as the legitimate outcome."[207] The *Twin Cities Pioneer Press* proved the point. Noting that it had enthusiastically endorsed Coleman, it declared that "the system worked. . . . Minnesota is blessed to have an impartial, competent, independent judiciary."[208] Professor Edward Foley, an election law expert who studied the case, succinctly captured the main takeaway from the Minnesota experience: "As in 1962, it was the selection of the three-judge panel that was the most important factor in the state's successful resolution of the election."[209]

If we think of Minnesota's 1962 and 2008 election disputes as the counterpoint to *Bush v. Gore*, and ask what lessons can be learned from the state's successful resolution of "tie" elections, Foley's conclusion warrants emphasis. It perhaps should go without saying, but an impartial decision-maker is essential to public acceptance of the verdict in a disputed election. A second lesson is that sometimes the process takes time. If one reason courts stumbled in *Bush v. Gore* was the time pressure, one reason the Minnesota process worked well was the willingness of the decision-makers to take months in order to make sure they got things right. That luxury is less available when it comes to the presidency, but mainly because of constitutional constraints that can be loosened by amendment. A final lesson is the value of transparency: Coleman's election contest was not only open to the public, but streamed on the internet. Such openness mitigates against bias or corruption and reduces suspicion.

The three-judge panels (selected by the attorneys in 1962 and by the Minnesota Supreme Court in 2008) lived up to the expectation of impartiality and were embraced by the public. However, that will not always be the case with a panel chosen after Election Day. In the midst of a contested election, people on one side or the other will likely be suspicious of whoever does the appointing and therefore of whomever he or she appoints. Minnesota got lucky. As suggested earlier, a preexisting board is the better way to go.

That said, a preexisting decision-making body does not solve all problems, as we shall now see. For, in addition to Minnesota's positive example of how to resolve a disputed election, we have a negative example on the federal level—not quite in the area of deciding an election, but in something related.

The Unsuccessful Commission on Presidential Debates

The national Commission on Presidential Debates ("CPD") is an analogue to the Presidential Election Review Board ("PERB") created by my proposed constitutional amendment. The Commission on Presidential Debates, like the envisioned PERB, was designed to produce presidential elections that conform to democratic ideals. We can think of the CPD and PERB as the alpha and omega of presidential elections: the CPD, a pre-election vehicle to ensure that the electorate can make an informed choice; PERB, a post-election vehicle to ensure that the people's choice is reliably determined.

The Commission on Presidential Debates arose from a combination of two realizations: 1) televised debates should be a permanent feature of presidential elections; and 2) left to their own devices, the candidates will often avoid such debates. Following the debut of presidential debates in 1960, there were no debates in 1964, 1968, and 1972, and only two incomplete debates were held in 1980. In 1964, 1968, and 1972, the front-runner (Lyndon Johnson in '64, Nixon in '68 and '72) perceived a risk and no advantage from participating in debates. In 1980, Jimmy Carter refused to participate when the sponsor, the League of Women Voters, invited independent candidate John Anderson as well as Carter and the

Republican nominee, Ronald Reagan. (Reagan and Anderson did debate once, and Reagan and Carter debated once as well, the latter occurring less than a week before the election when the League disinvited Anderson.)

Recognizing that the candidates held the debates hostage, a private group of influential Democrats and Republicans formed CPD, an independent nonprofit organization. The two major parties gave their blessing to CPD, and in 1988 it successfully sponsored two debates between presidential candidates George H.W. Bush and Michael Dukakis, as well as one between their running mates, Dan Quayle and Lloyd Bentsen. In 1992, CPD sponsored three three-way debates between Bush, Bill Clinton, and independent candidate Ross Perot, as well as one debate among their running mates. However, problems arose in 1996, when the Republican candidate, Bob Dole, believing that Perot had cost the Republicans the election in 1992, did not want him included in the debates. Eventually, the Dole and Clinton campaigns agreed to two debates that excluded Perot, and one vice-presidential debate that excluded Perot's running mate. George Will remarked that Perot's exclusion "actually was a deal struck by the Dole and Clinton campaigns," rather than a determination by CPD.[210]

Although presidential debates have taken place in every debate since, the '96 scenario exposed two major problems with the CPD. First, the commission is toothless. The Dole campaign simply rejected the invitations by the CPD, and instead privately arranged debates with the Clinton campaign. Ever since, the modus operandi of the national campaigns is to accept conditions proposed by CPD . . . when they feel like it. When it comes to the number and format of debates, as well as which candidates to include, each election produces a debate about debates in which CPD at most plays a mediating role. The commission's fatal flaw is that it lacks authority. It can only recommend and hope that the candidates accept its recommendations.

The second major problem with CPD is that it is bipartisan but not nonpartisan: It does the bidding of the major party candidates at the expense of third-party candidates and the public that might benefit from more inclusive debates. CPD's co-chairs and board members have always been Democrats and Republicans (many of them activists, donors, and former officeholders).[211] Its co-founders and long-standing co-chairs, Paul Kirk and Frank Fahrenkopf, were former chairs of the Democratic National Committee and Republican National Committee, respectively. They and other members of the CPD board have been forthright about their hostility toward third parties.[212]

The only time CPD invited a third-party candidate to debate—Perot in 1992—is the exception that proves the rule: The CPD did not want to invite Perot, and did so reluctantly only because Bush insisted.[213] In every election since, CPD has excluded third-party candidates. The 2000 campaign, for example, included two such candidates, Ralph Nader and Pat Buchanan, who had national followings and serious platforms. Many pundits and the public believed that their inclusion in at least one of the presidential debates would have enriched the discourse.[214] The CPD did not invite them.

The criteria established by CPD for inclusion in the debates are designed to ensure that third-party candidates will rarely qualify. Such candidates must, among other things, receive at least 15 percent of the vote in public opinion polls. This amounts to a self-denying prophecy, since third-party candidates will rarely poll at such levels unless given the opportunity to participate in debates with the Democratic and Republican candidates. But more forgiving criteria (such as a much lower threshold for inclusion in at least the first debate) will not be adopted as long as CPD is of, by, and for the two major parties. Recall that the three-judge panels that worked so well in deciding disputed elections in Minnesota were *tripartisan*, including someone not considered loyal to either major party.

When creating the Presidential Election Review Board (PERB), we should learn from the experience of Minnesota and CPD. We should prioritize avoiding the two major problems with CPD. Unlike CPD, PERB's decisions should be given, if not fully binding force, at least a favorable presumption. Also unlike CPD, PERB should include at least one member involved in the decision-making who is not affiliated with either the Democratic or Republican parties. In one key respect, PERB should emulate CPD: It should be established on a permanent basis, to avoid the pitfalls of an ad hoc approach to a disputed election.

Third parties should present little problem for PERB, especially if the Electoral College is maintained: No third-party candidate has captured a state in the last fifty years. Even without the Electoral College, third-party candidates are unlikely to figure directly in post-election disputes. Their disputed votes may affect the outcome, as when Florida's butterfly ballot gave Pat Buchanan votes intended for Al Gore, but Gore, not Buchanan, was the party adversely affected. Buchanan himself had zero chance of winning Florida. Third-party candidates rarely have a realistic chance of winning any states, much less the presidency.

Nevertheless, we should ensure that PERB is positioned to protect the interests of all candidates, not only the Democrat and Republican. After all, in 1992 Ross Perot received almost 19 percent of the vote, and before he dropped out of the race (only to rejoin it ten weeks later) was actually ahead in some polls.[215] In 1912, Theodore Roosevelt, running on the Bull Moose ticket, received 27.4 percent of the vote—more than the Republican candidate, Howard Taft. Because we cannot rule out a third-party candidate with a chance to win the presidency, at least one member of PERB should have no party affiliation.

The inclusion of one or more nonaffiliated PERB members will also serve another important purpose: Providing a third member avoids the risk of a voting deadlock without giving the Democrats or Republicans the extra member. But the inclusion of one nonpartisan member should not be used as an excuse to make the other members highly partisan. All members should have a reputation for independence and integrity. Current officeholders should be excluded because of the obvious conflict of interest.

The list of Democrats and Republicans who might pass muster today includes Joseph Lieberman, Jon Huntsman, Sam Nunn, Olympia Snowe, Colin Powell, Bill Richardson, Kay Bailey Hutchinson, William Cohen, Chuck Hegel, and Evan Bayh, among many other possibilities. The list of potential nonaffiliated members today includes James Mattis, Lowell Weicker, Jim Lehrer, David Boren, Richard Lamb, and Michael Bloomberg. (Needless to say, these lists are illustrative and not remotely exhaustive.) Note that many of these people have a legal background, which could be valuable insofar as contested elections often involve questions of statutory interpretation.

There will be presidential elections in which we do not immediately know the winner. That, alone, does not a crisis make. The crisis arises when we do not know who will decide the winner, or how that decision will be made. Such crises are preventable. Consider the following proposed constitutional amendment that simultaneously abolishes the Electoral College and establishes a Presidential Election Review Board.

CONSTITUTIONAL AMENDMENT 28

Section 1 On the Tuesday after the first Monday of November of the presidential election year, voters nation-wide shall cast a ballot for the ticket of president and vice president. The vote tabulations will be submitted to Congress by each voting location at the earliest possible date but no later than January 13, unless the date for inauguration is postponed in accordance with the procedures described below. Congress shall tabulate the total vote no later than January 13. The candidates on the ticket receiving the most votes shall be elected President and Vice President, provided that the ticket receives 40 percent or more of the total votes cast. The winners shall take office on January 20 unless the date for inauguration is postponed in accordance with the procedures described below. All reference to "Electors" in Article II is hereby inoperative.

Section 2 Congress shall establish a Presidential Election Review Board (PERB) for the purpose of resolving disputes concerning the winner of the presidential election. PERB shall consist of three members, who shall hold their offices during good behavior. Two of the members shall be registered members of the two political parties with the greatest number of registered members nationwide, with one member each belonging to each such party. A third member shall not be a member of either of those parties. Congress shall select the original three members, with two-thirds of each House required to agree on each member. When death, resignation, or removal creates a vacancy on the Board, the remaining members shall select the person to fill that vacancy. The new member shall have the same political affiliation or lack of affiliation as the person replaced.

Section 3 In the event that no ticket receives 40 percent of the vote, a runoff will take place between the top two finishers on a date determined by PERB but not later than December 1.

Section 4 If at any time prior to January 20, one of the losing candidates petitions PERB, stating under penalty of perjury the basis for a good faith belief that the election results are or will be inaccurate, and the error(s) may be sufficient to affect the outcome of the election, PERB will review the petition. By majority vote, PERB will determine whether the alleged good faith and sufficiency of error exists and requires further action.

Section 5 Upon a finding of good faith and sufficiency, PERB may declare that, in order to have sufficient time to conduct an investigation to determine the winner, the presidential inauguration will be postponed beyond January 20. The incumbent president shall remain in office during the period beyond January 20 and prior to the new inauguration date. Thereafter, PERB will conduct an investigation, which includes full subpoena power, and resolve all disputes necessary to determine the winner of the election.

Section 6 If PERB concludes that the winner cannot be determined, it will explain the reason for that determination and call for a re-vote either of the entire nation or of select precincts in which voter tabulation problems were identified. It will establish the date of the re-vote, though this date may not be less than one week or more than one month from the date of PERB's determination.

Section 7 If, at some point after the President has been inaugurated, PERB concludes that fraud took place sufficient to have affected the outcome of the election, it will explain the reason for that determination and, absent a determination of unusual circumstances precluding a remedy, shall call for a special election. It will establish the date of the election, though this date may not be less than one month from the date of PERB's determination. Unless Section 8 of this amendment applies, the ballot shall include the same candidates whose names appeared on the ballot during the previous presidential election.

Section 8 The political parties may petition PERB to replace the name of the candidate in the previous election with the name of a different candidate. Upon a finding of good cause, PERB may grant the request. Good cause requires a finding that the candidate listed is unavailable through death, illness, or other extraordinary circumstance including the candidate's removal from the ballot by PERB upon a finding that the candidate committed fraud.

Section 9 All determinations by PERB shall be binding and unreviewable in any court. However, Congress may reverse a determination by PERB if two-thirds of the members in each house find that it is arbitrary and capricious.

Section 10 All hearings held by PERB shall be open to the public.

Section 11 The Congress shall have power to enforce this article by appropriate legislation.

Obviously, the precise content of this proposed amendment can be changed in ways large and small. For example, while Section 11 specifically empowers Congress to implement and fund PERB, a provision might be added that would insulate PERB from politically motivated de-funding. So too, the provisions dealing with a special election or re-vote might address the treatment of absentee ballots in such elections. And, as long as we're remaking the presidential election, we should strongly consider tweaking aspects of the system unrelated or only peripherally related to the Electoral College and PERB, such as establishing Election Day as a national holiday or moving it to the weekend, so as to facilitate greater voter participation.

At this preliminary stage, we need not get deep into those weeds. What matters is the basic purpose and substance of the proposed amendment: In addition to replacing the Electoral College with a nationwide popular vote, it would establish a permanent body fully empowered to resolve presidential election disputes. Three features of the proposed amendment may raise eyebrows, and warrant elaboration: 1) the potential remedies of a re-vote and special election; 2) the provision allowing PERB to push back the date of a president's inauguration (even in cases not requiring a re-vote); and 3) the provision for Congress to override decisions made by PERB by a two-thirds vote of each House.[216]

Under the status quo, a re-vote is unavailable or at least impractical. After it became apparent that the butterfly ballot in Palm Beach cost Al Gore Florida and thus the presidency, several Palm Beach residents brought suit, urging a re-vote in either Palm Beach or the entire state. A Florida court held that the Constitution forbids such a remedy, and Florida's Supreme Court affirmed the decision.[217] Most commentators agreed with the decision.[218] While there have been re-votes on many occasions on the local level (in February 2019, the North Carolina Board of Elections ordered a new election for a congressional seat based on apparent fraud in the November 2018 election) and occasionally even in statewide elections, the presidential election is different because of the constitutional requirement that everyone vote on the same day. Article II, Section 1, Clause 4 stipulates that the day electors vote "shall be the same throughout the United States."[219]

Of course, the Constitution is referring to the votes

in the Electoral College, not the votes (or appointment process) that would select electors. That distinction may collapse, however, when we consider the situation in 1787. For the founders, where the election of the presidency was concerned, the Electoral College was the main event. Everything that happened before then was mere window dressing: The electors would meet and, exercising independent judgment, cast the only votes for president. Accordingly, the Constitution's stipulation that electors nationwide meet on the same day conceivably carries over to the votes for president that today are the main event—the vote by the American citizenry (with the Electoral College usually a formality to ratify the people's choice).

Seen this way, the fact that re-votes have happened in many state or local elections presents no precedent for presidential elections. If a state or municipality holds a re-vote for a statewide or local office, voters still vote on the same day—twice. But if only Florida (or only Palm Beach) re-voted in 2000, that would have violated the notion of everyone voting on the same day. Besides, the Constitution does not prescribe the rules governing state or local elections. It does prescribe some rules governing presidential elections. It is at least a plausible reading of the Constitution that any re-vote has to apply to the entire nation.

There is a policy basis supporting such a requirement. If only one state holds a re-vote, voters of that state will have information that no other voters had, specifically how the other forty-nine states had voted. Had Florida held a re-vote in 2016, for example, its voters would have known that the state's outcome would determine the nation's. Presumably many Nader voters would have defected to Gore. Granted, this is simply one of numerous contingencies that would have arisen because of the faulty first vote, and we could not be certain which candidate would fare better in the do-over. Still, Bush would have justifiably felt cheated that Buchanan voters in states won narrowly by Gore would not get the same opportunity for a tactical change of vote.

Ultimately, however, the argument against a national re-vote, based on the Constitution, is unconvincing. It rests on the premise that the clause requiring electors to vote on the same day should today be understood to require that all U.S. citizens vote for president on the same day. But any such requirement has long been ignored by the states when it comes to absentee ballots and early voting. (All fifty states permit the former and most permit the latter.) These days, the exceptions practically swallow the rule, because early and absentee voting have become common phenomena. In 2016, the first votes for president were cast on September 29, six weeks before Election Day. Literally millions of people voted prior to Election Day.

But even if the Constitution prohibits presidential re-votes (whether partial or whole), my proposed amendment undoes the prohibition by authorizing the Presidential Election Review Board to call for a re-vote. This provision serves a major purpose. After the 2016 election, the question was asked: What if it were determined that foreign covert operations produced Trump's victory? Worse still, what if the Trump campaign knew about or assisted such efforts? Writing for the political website FiveThirtyEight, Political Science professor Julia Aazari addressed whether a re-vote could be ordered as a remedy. Her conclusion: "So, is there a process for dealing with a finding that in essence invalidates an election? When it comes to presidential elections, the answer is: not really. . . . When it comes to the possibility that the winning side colluded with a foreign power to influence the election outcome, the Constitution doesn't offer much in the way of a plan."[220]

Aazari actually understates the constitutional omission. For one thing, the Constitution doesn't offer *anything* in the way of a plan for addressing a post-election discovery of malfeasance, unless you count on electors pledged to the colluding candidate flipping (and this possibility requires that the wrongdoing be uncovered before the Electoral College meets). In addition, the Constitution's failure is not limited to situations of candidate misconduct, let alone situations involving collusion with a foreign power. The Constitution offers no mechanism for dealing with *any* difficulties in determining the winner of a presidential election, whether or not involving wrongdoing by the ostensible winner.

Just as the Constitution provides no provision for a re-vote prior to a president's inauguration, it includes no provision for a special election after a president's inauguration. A post-inauguration special election threatens governmental stability even more than a pre-inauguration re-vote. Nevertheless, my proposed amendment includes provision for a special election, because there needs to be a remedy if we learn that an election result was inaccurate after the president has taken office.[221] As a federal judge put it in a case claiming fraud in New York during the 1976 presidential election, "It is difficult to imagine a more damaging blow to public confidence in the electoral process than the election of a President whose margin of victory was provided by fraudulent registration or voting, ballot-stuffing or other illegal means."[222] So too, it is difficult to disagree with constitutional law theorist Ronald Dworkin that "it would be wrong to declare, as a flat rule, that no remedy is ever available for demonstrable and grave illegality in the electoral process."[223] Exactly so. A presidential re-vote or special election should be a last resort, because finality is important and the last thing we need is defeated candidates routinely demanding a do-over. (Our presidential campaigns last long enough as it is!) But there may be circumstances in which no alternative is acceptable.

Under current law, when the discovery of an election-determinative impropriety occurs after the president's inauguration, impeachment seems to be the only remedy—and wholly inadequate, for several reasons. First, the removal of the president via an impeachment trial requires two-thirds of the senate voting to convict.

Since it is extremely rare for either party to control two-thirds of the senate, conviction requires a degree of bipartisanship, precisely what tends to be missing when it comes to crisis elections. Second, as noted above, the flawed election may not result from the president's wrongdoing. Perhaps the president's aides participated in fraud without his or her knowledge. Or perhaps the president and presidential staff did nothing wrong, but an outsider hacked the election in their favor. Impeachment makes little sense in that scenario. Third, if the president did commit fraud, impeachment still fails to resolve the underlying problem. As Professor Aazari says, "Even if collusion revelations did lead to Trump's impeachment and removal from office, the process wouldn't really address the question of whether his election had been legitimate in the first place."[224] Indeed, the impeachment and removal of Donald Trump would make Mike Pence president—and Pence, too, would have been a beneficiary of the fraudulent election.

For these reasons, a national re-vote and special election must be available remedies. Anyone who doubts that there should ever be such a remedy ought to consider the hypothetical supplied by election law expert Richard Hasan: "Imagine a terrorist attack on Election Day, where only part of [the country] gets to cast a vote for President, and many people stay home out of fear of additional attacks."[225] In that circumstance, it seems inconceivable that anything but a re-vote would be considered sufficient. Ditto if a hurricane or other natural disaster made voting impossible for a nontrivial portion of the electorate.

The absence of a remedy to undo an illegitimate presidential election once the president is in office has always been problematic, and has become more so in the age of hacking, which may take months or longer to detect. As the successful recounts in Minnesota in 1962 and 2008 illustrate, even when the problems are detected early, and even if no re-vote is required, the process of figuring out who won a virtual tie election can take time if it is to be done well. (The fiasco in Florida in 2000 reinforces this conclusion by way of negative example.) In part for that reason, my proposed constitutional amendment authorizes PERB to push back the date of the president's inauguration. As Dworkin observes, "It makes no sense to demand that a breathtakingly close election be finally decided by any magic dates in December in order that a new president be chosen by January 20."[226]

The stipulation in the proposed amendment that the incumbent continue in office until the dispute is resolved mirrors a provision in Minnesota's constitution that provided stability during the long period of uncertainty following the 1962 gubernatorial race. The Minnesota Constitution provides that the term of the incumbent governor carries over until a replacement is "chosen and qualified." Accordingly, Governor Anderson served well into March until it was determined that he had been defeated.

Finally, I should say a word about the stipulation in the proposed constitutional amendment that a two-thirds vote of both houses of Congress may reverse a PERB determination. Although the composition of PERB ought to safeguard against partisanship, no governmental entity should be immune from checks and balances. The precise mechanism chosen here, the two-house two-thirds requirement, has precedence in the Constitution, specifically the Twenty-Fifth Amendment, which permits the temporary removal of the president if the vice president and a majority of the cabinet determine that he or she is unable to discharge their duties. The president may subsequently reclaim the powers of the office, unless the vice president and a majority of the cabinet protest and two-thirds of both houses of Congress determine that the president remains unfit. The Presidential Election Review Board's determinations about an election, like that of the president concerning his own fitness, deserve a strong favorable presumption. Since it is rare for either party to dominate both houses, some degree of bipartisanship will generally be needed for PERB's determination to be rejected.

While I have coupled my two proposals into a single constitutional amendment, for simplicity's sake and because they each reduce the risk of a post-election crisis, the two central reforms are not dependent on one another. Abolishing the Electoral College would, by itself, reduce the likelihood of an election called into question by alleged fraud, even if we did not establish something like a Presidential Election Review Board to address such crises as do arise. Conversely, if we abandon the goal of abolishing the Electoral College, the remainder of my proposed amendment, establishing PERB to resolve disputes, would, with some tweaking, stand on its own. Creation of a PERB would be a major step forward whether or not we retain the Electoral College.

Readers may have misgivings about many of the specific provisions I have proposed related to PERB, but there is no good reason to resist the creation of some version of PERB. No one, Democrat or Republican, people in small states or large, should oppose the establishment of a body to deal with presidential election disputes in a fair and timely fashion.

CONCLUSION

In the conclusion to *Hacking Elections Is Easy*, the authors observe that "we send Americans to Iraq and Afghanistan to risk life, limb and death in order to spread and defend democracy abroad, yet we can't even preserve the most sacred expression of the democratic process against enemies within our own borders."[227]

I am not qualified to assess whether the authors are right that the United States today is essentially defenseless against election hacking, but they are clearly correct that we insufficiently protect our most consequential election. Long before the age of hacking, the United States failed to take the necessary action to preserve the legitimacy of presidential elections. As a result, we have suffered crises of legitimacy, and have been fortunate to be spared worse. The risk of old forms of fraud, not to mention pure accident, has placed us at peril before. Now we know that avowed enemies of democracy are taking aim at our elections. History suggests that we stand a nontrivial chance of any given presidential election leading to a crisis, a risk surely enhanced by the persistent threat of hacking and other forms of sabotage. We ignore the risk at our peril.

Judge Posner notes "the failure of the Constitution

to prescribe a method for resolving disputes over electors," and shrewdly explains the difficulty of resolving such disputes within the current election framework:

> The short time between the election and the inauguration, the necessity under the conditions of modern U.S. government for a transition period before inauguration in order to enable the President-elect to organize the new administration and hit the ground running on Inauguration Day, the fact that the "old" Congress takes a Christmas recess and the new one is not sworn in until after the first of the year, and the structure of Congress with its two houses and hundreds of members and poor reputation for statesmanship—all these things together make a credible, expeditious resolution of a dispute over electors unlikely. . . . We need a constitutional amendment.[228]

Posner asserts that, to have any chance of adoption, the amendment should not involve the abolition of the Electoral College. However, he acknowledges that there have been serious pushes to abolish the Electoral College and concedes that abolition is not a "quixotic long-term goal. . . . The objection to abolition has less to do with considerations of feasibility than with the fact that . . . a convincing case for abolition has not yet been made."[229]

I have aimed to make that case, or at least to introduce a new argument to buttress the case others have made. However, the Electoral College has survived countless abolitionist efforts. Whether or not the movement for abolition is quixotic, it certainly faces an uphill climb. Accordingly, I should emphasize, as I did at the close of the previous chapter, that the two parts of my proposed constitutional amendment—abolition of the Electoral College and creation of a Presidential Election Review Board—are by no means mutually dependent. We can adopt one without the other.

If we learn from the crises that marred past presidential elections, we can adopt measures that will safeguard against recurrence. The overarching problem is the power of inertia. Reasonable remedies exist, provided that we take the problem seriously and overcome that inertia.

ACKNOWLEDGMENTS

First, special thanks to Greg Ruggiero for his belief in this project and his help in bringing it to fruition. Also to the following for reading and providing thoughtful comments: Eric Hirsch, Sarah Hirsch, Joni Hirsch, Marjorie Hirsch, Howard Shapiro, Chris Merkling, David Shipler, and Alan Morrison. Evan Caminker, as is his wont, went above and beyond, reading and commenting on multiple drafts. Their numerous suggestions, large and small, have enriched this project.

ABOUT THE AUTHOR

Alan Hirsch, Instructor in the Humanities and Chair of the Justice and Law Studies program at Williams College, is the author of numerous works of legal scholarship and many books, including *For the People: What the Constitution Really Says About Your Rights* (coauthored with Akhil Amar) and *Impeaching the President: Past, Present, and Future*. He received a J.D. from Yale Law School and a B.A. from Amherst College. His work has appeared in the *Washington Post, Los Angeles Times, Washington Times, Newsday*, and *Village Voice*. Hirsch also serves as a trial consultant and expert witness on interrogations and criminal confessions, testifying around the nation. He lives in Williamstown, Massachusetts.

ENDNOTES

1. Arthur Schlesinger Jr., "How to democratize American Democracy," in *A Badly Flawed Election*, ed. Ronald Dworkin (The New Press, 2002), 216.

2. *Papers of Alexander Hamilton*, ed. Harold Syrett (Columbia University Press, 1962), vol. 5, 248 (letter to James Wilson, January 25, 1789).

3. *Adams Family Correspondence*, eds. L.H. Butterfield et al., (Harvard University Press, 1963), vol. 11, 122 (letter from John Adams to Abigail Adams, January 5, 1796).

4. Tadahisa Kuroda, *The Origins of the Twelfth Amendment* (Greenwood Press, 1994), 71 (letter to Rufus King, February 15, 1787).

5. See Gordon Wood, *Friends Divided: John Adams and Thomas Jefferson* (Penguin, 2017), 279–319. Tellingly, in his book about the Jefferson-Adams relationship, Wood, the preeminent historian of the founding, titled his chapter on the Adams-Jefferson administration "The President vs. the Vice President."

6. Akhil Amar, *America's Constitution: A Biography* (Random House, 2005), 339.

7. *The Federalist Papers*, ed. Clinton Rossiter (New American Library, 1961), 412.

8. *Memoirs of John Quincy Adams*, ed. Charles Francis Adams (J.B. Lippincott, 1875), vol. 6, 95–96.

9. Don C. Seitz, *The "Also Rans": Men Who Missed the Presidency* (Thomas Crowell, 1928), 43.

10. *Memoirs of John Quincy Adams*, vol. 5, 361.

11. Ibid., vol. 6, 114.

12. James Hopkins, "Election of 1824" in *History of American Presidential Elections, 1789-1968*, ed. Arthur Schlesinger Jr. (Chelsea House, 1971), 360.

13. Ibid., 363.

14. Quoted in Donald Ratcliffe, *The One-Party Presidential Contest* (University Press of Kansas, 2015), 155.

15. *The Papers of Henry Clay*, ed. James Hopkins (University of Kentucky Press, 1963), vol. 3, 887 (letter to Francis T. Brooke, November 26, 1824).

16. Letter to George Hay, August 17, 1823, quoted in David K. Watson, *The Constitution of the United States: Its History, Application and Construction* (Callaghan & Co., 1910), vol. 2, 1579.

17. Hopkins, "Election of 1824," 377.

18. *Private Correspondence of Henry Clay* (Calvin Colton ed., A.S. Barnes & Co., 1856), vol. 4, 109-110 (letter to Francis Preston Blair, January 8, 1825).

19. *The Papers of Henry Clay*, vol. 3, 901 (letter to Benjamin Leigh, December 22, 1824).

20. Ibid., 895 (letter to James Erwin, December 13, 1824).

21. Ibid., vol. 4, 10 (letter to Francis Preston Blair, January 8, 1825).

22. Ibid., vol. 3, 906 (letter to George McClure, December 28, 1884).

23. Ibid., vol. 4, 39 (letter to James Brown, January 23, 1825) (emphasis in original.

24. *The Papers of Andrew Jackson*, eds. Sam Smith et al. (University of Tennessee Press, 1980), vol. 5, 121 (letter to James Gadsden, December 6, 1821).

25. *The Papers of Henry Clay*, vol. 4, 110 (letter to Francis Preston Blair, January 8, 1825).

26. Ibid., 10 (letter to Francis Preston Blair, January 8, 1825).

27. *Memoirs of John Quincy Adams*, vol. 6, 464–65.

28. Ibid., 465.

29. Calvin Colton, *The Life and Times of Henry Clay* (A.S. Barnes, 1846) , 385 (letter to Francis T. Brooke, January 28, 1825).

30. *Memoirs of John Quincy Adams*, vol. 6, 483.

31. *The Papers of Henry Clay*, vol. 3, 47 (letter to Francis Preston Blair, January 29, 1825).

32. *Memoirs of John Quincy Adams*, vol. 6, 484.

33. Ibid., 471.

34. Ibid., 491.

35. Ibid., 83.

36. Ibid., 447 (emphasis in original).

37. Ibid., 474.

38. *The Papers of Henry Clay*, vol. 4, 55 (February 4, 1825, letter to Francis T. Brooke).

39. *Memoirs of John Quincy Adams*, vol. 6, 496.

40. *Andrew Jackson papers*, eds. Harold Moser & Clint Cliff (University of Tennessee Press, 2002) vol. 6, 29–30 (letter to William B. Lewis, February 14, 1824).

41. *Memoirs of John Quincy Adams*, vol. 6, 26.

42. Ibid., 114.

43. Ibid., vol. 6, 501.

44. Ibid.

45. Ibid., 505.

46. Ibid., 506.

47. Ibid., 507.

48. Ibid., 508.

49. Ibid., 508.

50. Ibid., 514.

51. *The Papers of Henry Clay*, vol. 4, 73 (letter to Francis T. Brooke, February 18, 1825).

52. Ibid., 47 (letter to Francis Preston Blair, January 29, 1825).

53. *The Papers of Henry Clay*, vol. 3, 906 (letter to George McClure, December 28, 1824).

54. A caveat must be attached. The Constitution allows each state to determine the method by which its electors are chosen. Today, of course, all states do so by a popular election open to all eligible voters. In 1824, however, only 18 of the 24 states did so. Jackson's overall "landslide" numbers are based on the tallies from those states. In six states, however, the electors were chosen by the state legislature. That includes New York, a populous state where Adams was allegedly favored by most voters. Had New York and the other five states held popular elections, Adams's overall vote total might have approached or even exceeded Jackson's. See Michael J. Korzi, "'If the Manner of It Be Not Perfect': Thinking Through Electoral College Reform," in *Electoral College Reform: Challenges and Possibilities*, ed. Gary Bugh (Routledge, 2010), 48 n. 19 (arguing that we can't really say who won the popular vote in 1824).

55. *Memoirs of John Quincy Adams*, vol. 6, 496.

56. David Jordan, *Roscoe Conkling of New York: Voice in the Senate* (Cornell University Press, 1972), 421.

57. The incident is recounted in David Saville Muzzey, *James G. Blaine: A Political Idol of Other Days* (Kennikat Press, 1963), 99–100.

58. Letter to R.B. Buckland, June 14, 1876, quoted in Keith Polakoff, *The Politics of Inertia: The Election of 1876 and the End of Reconstruction* (Louisiana State University Press, 1973), 56.

59. Ibid., 67 (letter to Carl M. Gaskell, June 14, 1876).

60. Hans L. Trefousse, *The American Presidents Series: Rutherford B. Hayes: The 19th President* (Holt, 2002), 68.

61. *Chicago Daily News*, November 8, 1876.

62. For a collection of such declarations, see Roy Morris Jr., *Fraud of the Century* (Simon and Schuster, 2003), 164.

63. Michael Holt, *By One Vote: The Disputed Presidential Election of 1876* (University Press of Kansas, 2008), 180.

64. Norman J. Ornstein, "Three Disputed elections," in *After the People Vote: A Guide to the Electoral College*, ed.Walter Bernstein (AEI Press, 1992), 41.

65. H.R. Misc. Doc. No 45-31, at 1363 (1878).

66. For specifics, and a detailed analysis, see Edward Foley, *Ballot Battles: The History of Disputed Elections in the United States* (Oxford University Press, 2016), 120–123.

67. At least one historian reported the rumors as fact. See Polakoff, *The Politics of Inertia*, 213.

68. William H. Rehnquist, *Centennial Crisis* (Knopf, 2002), 112.

69. Paul Haworth, *The Hayes-Tilden Election* (Bobbs Merrill, 1906), 200.

70. Milton Harlow Northrup, "The Inner History of the Origin and Formation of the Electoral Commission of 1877," *XL Century* (1901), 927.

71. For example, on January 24, Hayes's political ally, William Henry Smith, wrote to Hayes, "Davis elected to the Senate by Democratic votes would feel under obligation, as the fifth judge, to give the Presidency to Tilden." Lally Weymouth & Milton Glazer, *America in 1876* (Random House, 1976), 35. There is some evidence that Tilden's adventurous nephew, William T. Pelton (but not Tilden himself), played a role in securing Davis the senate seat. See Holt, *By One Vote*, 220.

72. Hewitt, "Secret History of the Disputed Election, 1876–77," in *Selected Writings of Abram S. Hewitt*, ed. Allan Nevins (Kennikat, 1965), 171.

73. *New York Sun*, January 1, 1877.

74. Quoted in Holt, *By One Vote*, 224.

75. Willard King, *Lincoln's Manager, David Davis* (Harvard University Press, 1960), 293 n. 23.

76. Charles Fairman, *History of the Supreme Court* (Macmillan, 1988), vol. 7, 132.

77. *New York Sun*, July 6, 1877.

78. Quoted in Morris, *Fraud of the Century*, 241.

79. For a balanced evaluation of the evidence concluding that the charges were likely false, see Rehnquist, *Centennial Crisis*, 187–200.

80. Reproduced in full in Holt, *By One Vote*, 263–64.

81. James Ford Rhodes, *History of the United States* (Norwood Press, 1906), vol. 7, 243.

82. Ibid., 264.

83. Quoted in Morris, *Fraud of the Century*, 174.

84. 17 Congressional Record 815 (1886).

85. Foley, *Ballot Battles*, 118.

86. It is unclear to what extent voter suppression took place. The U.S. Civil Rights Commission produced a report about the election, and "concluded that Florida's election was marred by 'significant and distressing barriers' put in the way of African Americans who were attempting to vote." Michael A Genovese, "This is Guatemala," in *Counting Votes*, ed. Robert Watson (University Press of Florida, 2004), 253. Jeffrey Toobin claims there is "no credible evidence of an organized attempt to discourage African-Americans from going to the polls" but notes that "a purge of the voting lists presents a more complex story" in *Too Close to Call* (Random House, 2002), 169. He is referring to a 1998 law aimed at removing ineligible voters from the voting list. Toobin acknowledges that mistakes in the program disproportionately affected African American voters, but says that the widespread claim that sloppy enforcement of the 1998 law disenfranchised thousands of black voters is baseless. It is more difficult to refute—or verify— Lani Guinier's contention that "antiquated voting technology, lack of trained clerks, and confusing

instructions in many counties adversely affected black voters' ability to cast a 'legal vote.'" Guinier, "And to the C Students, the Lessons of *Bush v. Gore*," in *A Badly Flawed Election*, 237.

87. Toobin, *Too Close to Call*, 66.

88. *McDermott v. Harris*, 2000 WL 1693713 (Fl. Cir. Ct. Nov. 14, 2000).

89. Charley Wells, *Inside Bush v. Gore* (University Press of Florida, 2013).

90. Ibid., 87.

91. Ibid., 91.

92. Alan Dershowitz, *Supreme Injustice: How the High Court Hijacked Election 2000* (Oxford University Press, 2001), 37.

93. Gore v. Harris, 773 So. 2d 524 (Fla. 2000).

94. 773 So. 2d 524 (Wells, C.J., dissenting).

95. See Ronald Dworkin, "The Phantom Toll Booth," in *A Badly Flawed Election*, ed. Dworkin (The New Press, 2002), 66. (Several states use the "intent of the voter" standard for recounts, "and the Supreme Court has now declared that they have all been acting—no doubt for many decades—unconstitutionally.")

96. *Bush v. Gore*, 531 U.S. 98, 109 (2000).

97. I hedge simply out of caution, but constitutional scholar Erwin Chemerinsky asserts that, when it comes to denying its own decision any precedential value, "*Bush v. Gore* is a first. I don't believe any prior Supreme Court has done something like this before." Quoted in Vincent Bugliosi, *The Betrayal of America: How the Supreme Court Undermined the Constitution and Chose Our President* (Thunder's Mouth Press, 2001), 113.

98. See, e.g., Richard Epstein, "'In such Manner as the Legislature may Direct': The Outcome in Bush v. Gore Defended," in *The Vote*, eds. Cass Sunstein & Richard Epstein (University of Chicago Press, 2001), 14. ("Any equal protection challenge to the Florida Recount Procedure quickly runs into insurmountable difficulties"). By contrast, Epstein believes that the Article II argument, adopted by only three Justices, was sound.

99. *Bush v. Gore*, 531 U.S. at 146 (Breyer, J., dissenting).

100. Michael W. McConnell, "Two and a Half Cheers for *Bush v. Gore*," in *The Vote*, 118 ("I do not find that explanation very persuasive"). As Professor Frank Michelman put it, "No legal

deadline posed a need for federal judges thus to preclude Florida's high court from speaking for itself on this matter." "Suspicion or the New Prince," in *The Vote*, 128 n. 12.

101. Yale Law Professor Jed Rubenfeld captured the perversity perfectly. To whom had the Court deferred about the safe harbor? "That's right: The Florida Supreme Court, that august authority to which the United States Supreme Court refused to defer on virtually any other point of law in the entire controversy. . . . But on the dispositive, count-ending, election-determining issue of the December 12 deadline, the majority's hands were regrettably tied by their respectful regard for the Florida Justices' unquestionable power to declare that date to be the deadline under Florida law. Unfortunately, there was one more little problem. The Florida justices had not declared December 12 to be the deadline." Jed Rubenfeld, "Not as Bad as Plessy, Worse," in *Bush v. Gore: The Question of Legitimacy*, ed. Bruce Ackerman (Yale University Press, 2002), 23.

102. *Bush v. Gore*, 531 U.S., at 111.

103. Ibid., at (Scalia, J., concurring)

104. Ibid., at (Stevens, J., dissenting). As Professor David Strauss put it, "It is true that the failure to grant a stay might have inflicted political damage on a Bush presidency; but granting a stay might have wholly deprived Vice President Gore of the presidency." "Bush v. Gore: What were they Thinking?" in *The Vote*, 190.

105. Justice Ginsburg indicated that electoral votes could be submitted as late as January 6, but that appears doubtful under federal law. The Constitution stipulates that electors must meet to give their votes on a day that must be "the same throughout the United States," and in 2000, that date was December 18.

106. John Allen Paulos, "We're Measuring Bacteria with a Yardstick," *New York Times*, November 22, 2000.

107. Wells, *Inside Bush v. Gore*, 123. Judge Richard Posner endorsed the Supreme Court's intervention on this ground. See "Florida 2000: A Legal and Statistical Analysis of the Election Deadlock and the Ensuing Litigation," 2000 *Supreme Court Review* 1, 45 ("I cannot see the case for precipitating a political and constitutional crisis merely in order to fuss with a statistical tie that cannot be untied").

108. For a shrewd critique of the consortium's findings, see Foley, *Ballot Battles*, 283-84.

109. In separate lawsuits alleging such unequal treatment in different counties, Judge Terry Lewis and Judge Nikki Clark both found some improper actions but no available remedy. *Jacobs v. Seminole County Canvassing Board*, 773 So. 2d 519 (Fla. 2000); *Taylor v. Martin County Canvassing Board*, 773 So. 2d 517 (Fla. 2000).

110. T.S. Eliot, *Murder in the Cathedral* (Harcourt Brace, 1935), 44.

111. As one election law expert says, "The Florida mess should have convinced both Democrats and Republicans that there is something wrong with having partisan election officials making discretionary decisions that could affect the outcome of a presidential election." Richard Hasen, "Beyond the Margin of Litigation: Reforming Election Administration to Avoid Electoral Meltdown," 62 *Washington & Lee Law Review* 937, 978 (2005).

112. *Bush v. Gore*, 531 U.S. at 111.

113. Those taking this position included respected conservative and liberal legal scholars alike. See, e.g., Steven Calabresi, "A Political Question," in *Bush v. Gore: The Question of Legitimacy*, 129-44; Erwin Chemerinsky, "Bush v. Gore was not Justiciable," 76 *Notre Dame Law Review* 1093 (2001).

114. As Professor Frank Michelman observed, "senators and representatives caring to retain their offices would have had to face the judgments of voters on their manner of settling the election. In the circumstances of this case, that is a tremendous advantage of institutional competency or fitness." Michelman, "Suspicion or the New Prince," in *The Vote*, 133.

115. Jeffrey Rosen, "The Supreme Court Commits Suicide," *The New Republic*, December 12, 2000.

116. 531 U.S. at 128-29 (Stevens, J., dissenting).

117. During the debate over the Electoral Count Act, passed a decade after the 1876 election, Congress considered empowering the Supreme Court to resolve future disputes. With the recollection fresh of the vilification of Justice Bradley for his role on the commission that resolved the '76 election, Senator John Sherman of Ohio shrewdly remarked that the Court's involvement "would tend to bring that court into public odium of one or the other of the two great parties." 17 *Congressional Record* 818 (1886).

118. Epstein, "Afterword" in *The Vote*, 243.

119. "Stephen Carter, "Time Doesn't Heal Wounds From Bush v. Gore," *The Morning Call*, January 8, 2019. Similarly, Alan Dershowitz writes that, in the wake of Bush v. Gore, he spoke to dozens of successful lawyers, and "virtually every one of them, Democrat or Republican, agrees with me that the majority of the Justices in the Florida election case fail the-shoe-on-the-other-foot test." *Supreme Injustice*, 171.

120. National Commission on Federal Election Reform, Final Report (2001), 60.

121. Foley, *Ballot Battles*, 307.

122. Ibid., 307, 308. It would not have helped that the electoral situation in Ohio was highly charged; the secretary of state was co-chair of the state's Bush campaign committee, and distrusted by Democrats. His decisions gave rise to litigation even before Election Day, and Democrats and Republicans both fielded large teams of lawyers to the state in anticipation of a dispute. See Hasen, "Beyond the Margin of Litigation," 62 *Washington & Lee Law Review* at 939–41.

123. Deb Riechmann & Russ Bynum, "Report Suggests Russia Hackers Breached Voting Software Firm; Contractor Arrested for Leaks," *Associated Press*, June 5, 2017.

124. David E. Sanger and Catie Edmondson, "Russia Targeted Election Systems in All Fifty States, Report Finds," *New York Times*, July 25, 2019.

125. Ibid.

126. *Report of the Select Committee on Intelligence, United States Senate, On Russian Active Measures Campaigns and Interference in the 2016 U.S. Election*, www.intelligence.senate.gov/sites/default/files/documents/Report_Volume1.pdf, 40.

127. Christopher Bing, "Exclusive: U.S. officials fear ransomware attack against 2020 election," Reuters, August 26, 2019, www.reuters.com/article/us-usa-cyber-election-exclusive/exclusive-us-officials-fear-ransomware-attack-against-2020-election-idUSKCN1VG222

128. Ibid.

129. Ibid.

130. Blaze et al., "Voting Village: Report on Cyber

Vulnerabilities in U.S. Election Equipment, Databases, and Infrastructure," *DEF CON 26*, September 2018, 4 (2018). www.defcon.org/images/defcon25/DEF%20CON%2025%20voting%20village%20report.pdf.

131. Ibid., 5.

132. *Hacking Elections Is Easy*, 72 (emphasis added).

133. National Academy of Sciences, Engineering, and Medicine, *Securing the Vote: Protecting American Democracy* (the National Academies Press, 2018), 86–87. Malware is only one potential source of attacks on elections. See ibid. (discussing other sources of attack).

134. See Julian E. Barnes and Adam Goldman, "FBI Warns of Russian Interference in 2020 Race and Boosts Counterintelligence Operations," *New York Times*, April 26, 2019.

135. See, e.g., Will Bunch, "Did Russian hackers make 2016 NC voters disappear? Why won't we stop this for 2020?" *Philadelphia Inquirer*, June 20, 2019. ("U.S. election systems could be every bit as vulnerable to outside monkey business in the 2020 presidential election, because Senate Majority Leader Mitch McConnell and his GOP lawmakers are refusing to vote on critical election security bills that would provide federal dollars and support to local election systems to upgrade cybersecurity, as well as requiring paper ballots and audits that would ensure the integrity of the vote.")

136. Ibid.

137. Patricia Mazzei, "FBI to Florida Lawmakers: 'You Were Hacked by Russians, but Don't Tell Voters,'" *New York Times*, May 16, 2019.

138. Erin Tucker & Colleen Long, "U.S. Officials Say Foreign Election Hacking Is Inevitable," *Associated Press*, May 19, 2019.

139. Quoted in Steven Hendrix, *The New Nicaragua, Lessons in Nation-building, Development, and Democracy for the United States* (Praeger, 2009), 11.

140. Bennett, *Taming the Electoral College*, 187.

141. Mark Mazzetti, "Mueller Warns of Russian Sabotage and Rejects Trump's 'Witch Hunt' Claims," *New York Times*, July 24, 2019.

142. Tami Abdollah, "Iranian Hackers Said to Target Presidential Campaign," *Associated Press*, October 4, 2019.

143. Because the 1800, 1824, and 1876 elections were ultimately

resolved by backroom deals, it is worth noting that some Founding Fathers considered such shenanigans a foreseeable result of the Electoral College. See Michael T. Rogers, "'A Mere Deception—a Mere Ignus Fatus on the People of America': Lifting the Veil on the Electoral College," in *Electoral College Reform*, 35–38.

144. Akhil Amar, "President Thurmond?" *Slate*, November 2, 2000.

145. As Professor Robert Bennett has observed, the risk of a tie could be greatly reduced simply by adding one member to the House of Representatives (and thus to the Electoral College) to produce an odd number. *Taming the Electoral College* (Stanford University Press, 2006), 182.

146. Amar, "President Thurmond?"

147. Lawrence Longley & Neal Peirce, *The Electoral College Primer* (Yale University Press, 1996), 135–36.

148. See, e.g., Michael Herz, "How the Electoral College Imitates the World Series," 23 *Cardozo Law Review* 1191 (2002).

149. Pressed by a congressman about the World Series analogy, Professor Akhil Amar replied: "It does not matter very much who wins the World Series. So the arbitrariness of certain rules that define a game is less troubling if, in the end, the game is just a game." "Proposals for Electoral College Reform," *Hearings on H.J. Res. 28 and H.J. Res. 43 Before the Subcommittee on the Constitution of the House Committee on the Judiciary*, 105th Cong. 78 (1997).

150. As for the framers' esoteric ideas about the Electoral College, we need to be careful. The framers had no clear expectations for the Electoral College, the creation of which was largely motivated by the need to avoid something worse. See Rakove, "The E-College in the E-Age," 201–34.

151. "Direct Popular Election of the President and Vice President of the United States," Hearings on S.J. Resolution 28 Before the Subcommittee on the Constitution of the Senate Committee on the Judiciary, 96th Cong. 2-3 (1979).

152. At least to some extent, the framers saw the Electoral College as a buffer against the tendency of ordinary people to make unwise decisions based on passion, whereas electors, an elite group, were more likely to choose the president based on public-spirited reasoning. Thus, the Electoral College would minimize

the likelihood of the election of a popular scoundrel or ignoramus. However, today the electors essentially rubber-stamp a decision made by the full electorate, and thus don't serve this major role the founders imagined them playing. For a succinct summary of the various differences between the Electoral College as the founders envisioned and how it works today, see Bennett, *Taming the Electoral College*, 186.

153. Akhil Amar, "The Electoral College, Unfair from Day One," *New York Times*, November 9, 2000.

154. George C. Edwards, *Why the Electoral College Is Bad for America* (Yale University Press, 2004), 107.

155. See, e.g., Garry Wills, *Negro President: Jefferson and the Slave Power* (Houghton Mifflin, 2003). One prominent historian who had seen things the same way recently recanted. See Sean Wilentz, "The Electoral College Was Not a Pro-Slavery Ploy," *New York Times*, April 4, 2019.

156. Maine Beacon, "LePage claims national popular vote bill will silence 'white people,'" *Maine Beacon*, February 28, 2019, mainebeacon.com/lepage-claims-national-popular-vote-bill-will-silence-white-people/.

157. The Records of the Federal Convention of 1787 (ed. Max Farrand, Yale University Press 1911), vol. 2, 57.

158. Akhil Reed Amar, "The Troubling Reason the Electoral College Exists," *Time Magazine*, November 8, 2018, updated November 26, 2018.

159. See Rogers, "'A Mere Deception," in *Electoral College Reform*, 28 ("Those supporting direct popular election were a sizable faction at the [Constitutional] Convention"). Rogers also notes that there was substantial criticism of the Electoral College in the state ratifying conventions. Ibid., 30.

160. Article V of the Constitution, which sets forth the process for amending the Constitution, provides that "no state, without its consent, shall be deprived of its equal suffrage in the senate."

161. See Bennett, *Taming the Electoral College*, 60 ("The electoral college introduces a state-centered element in presidential selection, thus arguably compromising the national focus of the presidency."). For an in-depth argument that the Electoral College does not

promote federalism, see Edwards, *Why The Electoral College Is Bad for America*, 115–22.

162. Moreover, the actual effects of the Electoral College in terms of the influence of small states is more complicated than it might seem. See Amar, *The Constitution Today* (Basic Books, 2016), 347 ("The electoral college privileges small states by giving every state three electoral votes at the start. . . . But the college also exaggerates the power of big states, via winner-take-all primaries.").

163. See Richard Posner, *Breaking the Deadlock* (Princeton University Press, 2010) (showing that Gore's margin was beyond any recount), 225.

164. Martin Diamond, "The Electoral College and the American Idea of Democracy" (American Enterprise Institute, 1977), reproduced in *After the People Vote*, 61. See also Robert M. Hardaway, *Crisis at the Polls: An Electoral Reform Handbook* (Greenwood, 2008), 66.

165. There have been, to be sure, any number of elections in which the winning candidate's margin in the Electoral College was, on a percentage basis, much greater than their margin in the popular vote. But these have been, with few exceptions, cases of a landslide seeming like an even greater landslide. For example, in 1988 George Bush received 53.4 percent of the popular vote and 79 percent of the Electoral College vote. More extreme still, in 1972 Richard Nixon received 60 percent of the popular vote and 96 percent of the electoral votes, and in 1984 Ronald Reagan received 58.5 percent of the popular vote and 98 percent of the electoral vote. In general, the bigger the landslide, the greater this amplifying effect of the Electoral College. But in landslides, no amplification is necessary.

166. Longley & Peirce, *The Electoral College Primer*, 36.

167. Professor Judith Best shrewdly argues that "the shift-in-votes argument doesn't work because voters aren't numbers, and you can't just shift a few of them from one column to another without explaining what would have caused this shift by only these voters and not other voters in other states." *The Choice of the People? Debating the Electoral College* (Rowman & Littlefield, 1996), 27. However, Professor Best makes this argument in response to the

"wrong winner" argument, not the "fraud" argument. Note that we have indeed explained what could cause a shift in just a few states—hackers targeting swing states. As respects the wrong winner argument, it should also be noted that Best's book was published in 1996. She refuted the wrong winner argument in large part by observing that a candidate winning the Electoral College despite losing the popular vote "occurs very rarely and only in an election that verges on a tie." However, this subsequently occurred twice in 16 years, and the second time in an election where the loser's lead in the popular vote was close to three million votes.

168. It has been apparent for some time that this claim turns reality on its head. Writing in 2004, Professor George Edwards made the point I am making. He remarked that, following the 1960 election, Republicans cited voting irregularities affecting a few thousand votes in a few counties in Illinois and Texas that they believed might have been decisive. Edwards responds: "These suspicious circumstances occurred *under the electoral college.* Conversely, under direct election of the president, it would typically require a large change in votes to alter the national outcome—even if the electoral vote had been very close. . . . Direct election would create a *disincentive* for fraud, because altering an election outcome through fraud would require an organized effort of proportions never witnessed in the United States. And because no one in any state could know that his or her efforts at fraud would make a difference in the election, there would be little reason to risk trying." *Why the Electoral College Is Bad for America*, 124 (emphasis in original). See also Longley & Peirce, *The Electoral College Primer,* 69 ("The electoral college also encourages fraud—or at least fear and rumor of fraud").

169. James Scott & Drew Spaniel, *Hacking Elections Is Easy: Preserving Democracy in the Digital Age* (Institute for Critical Structure Technology, 2016), 3.

170. See Tara Ross, *The Indispensable Electoral College* (Regnery Gateway, 2017), 43. ("Assuming the election is close, dishonest actors must be able to predict which state (or states) will be close enough to influence the final results. This is harder than it sounds.")

171. Indeed, data suggest that voter turnout is higher in

battleground states than non-battleground states. See Thomas Neale & Andrew Nolan, "The National Popular Vote Initiative: National Popular Vote and Electoral College Options," in *Proposals for Presidential Election Reform* (ed. Maureen Stone, Nova, 2015), 15.

172. See Posner, *Breaking the Deadlock* ("The probability of a tie decreases with the number of votes cast"), 229; Herz, "How the Electoral College Imitates the World Series," 1212 (noting that in 2000, unlike in Florida, "the national election was *not* excruciatingly close, nor is it likely ever to be simply because the electorate is so large").

173. As Professor Richard Hasen puts it, "The popular vote method increases the vote margin between candidates, because it aggregates votes from all fifty states plus the District of Columbia. Even in an extremely close popular vote race in percentage terms, the absolute numbers on a national scale would be difficult to overcome through litigation." Hasen, "Beyond the Margin of Litigation," 948. While stating that "it is hard to reach this conclusion with any confidence," Hasen agrees with my premise: "Abolition of the Electoral College probably would decrease the potential for meltdown."

174. Jack Rakove, "The E-College in the E-Age," in *The Unfinished Election of 2000*, ed. Rakove (Basic Books, 2001), 226.

175. Richard Posner, *Breaking the Deadlock*, 235.

176. Ibid., 234.

177. Ibid., 239.

178. Ibid., 234.

179. Professor Richard Epstein succinctly concedes my point while making Posner's: "The odds of a national recount for [the] popular vote seem small, but the turmoil such a recount could create seems too large." *The Vote*, 246. It may be a mistake to focus on the *quantity* of confusion posed by a national recount and therefore conclude that the situation is qualitatively worse than when a recount is confined to a single state. There will be more sites of recounts and perhaps more confusion and litigation, but the outcome can hardly be worse than what happened in Florida in 2000, when half the country felt cheated—not without reason—by the resolution.

180. One additional advantage of abolishing the Electoral College is that doing so would necessarily also abolish the "contingent election"—the House of Representatives picking a winner when no candidate receives a majority of the electoral votes. Though this has happened only once, in 1824 (not counting the 1800 election that preceded and occasioned the Twelfth Amendment), the outcome of that election, where the legitimacy of the winner was tainted by suspicions of a "corrupt bargain," suffices to discourage any desire for a repeat.

181. As one longtime advocate of proportioning electoral votes says, "Clearly, splitting electoral votes reflects preferences of voters within the state better when compared to the winner-take-all system." Vincy Fon, "Integral Proportional System: Aligning Electoral Votes More Closely with State Popular Votes," 16 *Supreme Court Economic Review* 127 (2008).

182. For a shrewd discussion of proportionate allocation, see James Corey, "The 2000 Presidential Election: Is There a Better Way of Determining the Election Outcome?" in *Counting Votes*, 159–68. Watson also considers a "district plan" that would award the winner of the state two electoral votes, and give one electoral vote each to the winner of each congressional district in the state.

183. Bennett, *Taming the Electoral College*, 148. For an elaboration on this perspective, see Best, *The Choice of the People*, 10–15.

184. If proportional allocation were implemented, we would need some mechanism to handle the so-called "rounding problem." Consider the various states that have only three electoral votes. If Candidate A receives 52 percent of the popular vote in such a state, and Candidate B 40 percent, what is the fair allocation? To award Candidate A two of the three electoral votes is to give them 67 percent of the vote in that state, even though they received a much smaller percentage among actual voters. Nor does such a problem arise only in states with an odd number of electoral votes. Think of a state with four electoral votes, and one candidate winning 60 percent of the vote. Here, too, no fair proportional allocation is possible.

185. See Korsi, "If the Manner Be Not Perfect," in *Electoral*

College Reform ("Given the high value that democratic theory places on political participation, this is seen as one of the most serious drawbacks to the Electoral College"), 51.

186. See Rakove, "The E-College in the E-Age," in *The Unfinished Election of 2000*, 219–20.

187. The perception that an amendment would be needed would help explain why the Electoral College has survived. It has never been popular with the American people. See, e.g., Sarah Dutton et al., "Poll: More Americans Believe Popular Vote Should Decide the President," www.cbsnews.com, December 19, 2016; Lydia Saad, "Americans Call for Term Limits, End to Electoral College," www.gallup.com/159881/americans-call-term-limits-end-electoral-college.aspx (2013). The Gallup Poll in 2013 found that 63 percent of Americans favored a constitutional amendment to establish direct election of the President. The American people have preferred ending the Electoral College from as far back as the question has been polled. See Schlesinger, "How to Democratize American Democracy," in *A Badly Flawed Election*, 221 (citing Gallup Polls going back to 1944).

188. For a balanced look at NPVIC's strengths and weaknesses, see Thomas Neale and Andrew Nolan, "The National Popular Vote Initiative: Direct Election of the President by Interstate Compact," in *The National Popular Vote Initiative. Proposals for Presidential Election Reform*, ed. Maureen Stone, (Nova, 2015), 1–40.

189. Akhil Amar says no, because NPVIC does not create a new governmental apparatus and merely commits each state signatory to exercise power it could exercise on its own. "Some Thoughts on the Electoral College: Past, Present, and Future," 33 *Ohio Northern University Law Review* 467 (2007), 478. See also Bennett, *Taming the Electoral College*, 170–74.

190. For discussion of whether the congressional endorsement requires explicit congressional action, see Neale & Nolan, in *Proposals for Presidential Election Reform*, 24.

191. For example, voters could be asked to record their second and third preferences (as well as first), effectively incorporating a run-off into the original vote. See Vikram Amar, "The Case for

Reforming Presidential Elections by Subconstitutional Means: The Electoral College, the National Popular Vote Compact, and Congressional Power," 100 *Georgetown Law Journal* 237 (2011–12). As long as we're engaging in such speculation, it is also worth pointing out that there is another means by which a national popular vote to determine the presidency could be achieved. We have discussed an interstate agreement as an alternative to a constitutional amendment, but as Akhil Amar observes, we needn't depend on either method. To move from the Electoral College to a national popular vote, all we need is an agreement between two people: the presidential candidates themselves. An agreement between them to instruct their electors to cast their ballot for the candidate who receives the most votes nationwide would help bring about the election of that candidate. See Amar, *The Constitution Today*, 355–57. What if the electors ignored the candidates' request, i.e., Candidate A's electors voted for A even though the candidate instructed them not to? Candidate A would have the last word: They could resign the office once elected. To ensure that Candidate B, and not Candidate A's running mate, attained the office, is admittedly a bit trickier. See ibid., 356–57.

192. See Akhil Amar, "Electoral College Reform, Lincoln-Style," 112 *Northwestern University Law Review* 63, 76 (2017). "The uniform and interlocking state laws enacted under the NPVIC will need to be supplemented by a comprehensive congressional statute providing detailed federal oversight of the presidential election process in all states—not merely the states that enact the NPVIC law."

193. See Bennett, *Taming the Electoral College*, 156. "The 2000 election also taught us that the 'normal' is not always what we get. We should prepare for the abnormal."

194. To be sure, efforts have been under way for some time to make our election machinery less vulnerable. See ibid., 88. However, while touting such efforts, the National Academy of Sciences, Engineering, and Medicine acknowledges that "there is no realistic mechanism to fully secure vote casting and tabulation computer systems from cyber threats." Ibid., 92.

195. Some experts on the Electoral College endorse the January

6 date. See Bugliosi, *The Betrayal of America*, 109 (quoting Professor L. Kinvin Wroth, who has written and testified about the Electoral College).

196. Julian M. Pleasants, *Hanging Chads* (Palgrave Macmillan, 2004), 248.

197. Ibid.

198. Ibid., 269.

199. For discussion of Harris's background and conduct throughout the recount saga, see Martin Merzer et al., *The Miami Herald Report: Democracy Held Hostage* (Miami Herald Publishing Co., 2001), 133–54.

200. Professor Foley independently arrived at a similar proposal. See Foley, *Ballot Battles*, 355 (Congress should pass "a simple procedure that empowers an impartial Electoral Count Tribunal to adjudicate any dispute that arises. . . .") Foley calls his proposed board an Electoral Count Tribunal, because he presupposes the continued existence of the Electoral College, and he calls for a statute rather than a constitutional amendment. By contrast, I would like to see the commission created by a constitutional amendment that also abolishes the Electoral College. There are various other differences between our proposals, such as the number of members on the commission, who selects them, how long they serve, and the margin needed in Congress to override their determinations. I would also give the board more power to enact a greater range of remedies. These differences notwithstanding, I find it encouraging that Professor Foley and I, having studied the history of crisis elections, arrived at similar mechanisms for preventing repeats. Foley also headed an American Law Institute (ALI) project that in part sought a better approach to resolving disputed elections. See *Principles of the Law, Election Administration: Non-precinct Voting and Resolution of Ballot-Counting Disputes* no. 2 (April 19, 2017). ALI recommends that each state establish a Presidential Election Court (PEC) consisting of three judges appointed prior to the election by the secretary of state or whoever is responsible for administering elections in that state. PEC differs from the PERB I propose in various particulars, including one crucial matter that stems in part from my opposition to the Electoral College: PEC operates within each state, whereas PERB is a federal board. This contributes to

other differences. For example, ALI would make PEC decisions appealable to the state supreme court, whereas I propose that PERB decisions can be reversed only by the U.S. Congress. Here, the issue is more than state-federal. I avoid the normal court system in part because the courts, too, are often considered partisan. While my goal of avoiding partisanship may seem directly at odds with my provision for Congress as the ultimate arbiter, I stipulate that PERB decisions can be reversed only by *two-thirds of each House*. Thus, I seek the best of both worlds, placing ultimate responsibility in the hands of a body accountable to the people but in a way that will generally respect PERB decisions absent a bipartisan determination of error. In any event, notwithstanding the major differences between ALI's proposal and mine (especially my effort to nationalize the election and therefore the election review process), our approaches are broadly congruent, both seeking to create a preexisting, impartial decision-making process to resolve disputed presidential elections.

201. For the best account of that election, and one I rely on as well in connection with the 2008 election for U.S. senator from Minnesota, see Foley, *Ballot Battles*, 238–46 and 318–36. For the 2008 election, I also found indispensable Jay Weiner, *This Is Not Florida: How Al Franken Won the Minnesota Senate Recount* (University of Minnesota Press, 2010).

202. "Minnesota's Close Election," *Washington Post*, March 26, 1963.

203. Wiener, *This Is Not Florida*, 14.

204. *Coleman v. Ritchie* (2008) (Page, J., dissenting), 58 N.W.2d 306, 311 (2008) (Page, J., dissenting).

205. Quoted in Wiener, *This Is Not Florida*, 194, 208.

206. "The Absentee Senator," *Wall Street Journal*, July 2, 2009.

207. "A Gracious Finish to an Epic Drama," *Minnesota Star Tribune*, June 30, 2009.

208. "At Long Last," *Twin Cities Pioneer Press*, June 30, 2009.

209. Foley, *Ballot Battles*, 326.

210. George Will, "Make Way for Buchanan," *Washington Post*, September 21, 1999.

211. Third-party candidates and independent organizations have brought legal action (unsuccessfully) in an effort to open up the

debates to more candidates. In the most recent such case, *Level the Playing Field vs. Federal Election Commission*, 232 F. Supp. 130 (D. D. C. 2017), the Court noted that Paul Kirk, a Democrat and longtime co-chair of CPD, "has stated that he personally believed the CPD should exclude third-party candidates from the debates," 232 F. Supp. at 134.

212. See, e.g., George Farah, *No Debate: How the Republican and Democratic Parties Secretly Control the Presidential Debates* (Seven Stories Press, 2004), 9–10.

213. Ibid., 48–54.

214. See ibid., 105 (noting a Fox News Poll, released on July 12, 2000, finding that 64 percent of respondents wanted Buchanan and Nader included in the debates).

215. See E. J. Dionne, "Perot Leads Field in Poll," *Washington Post*, June 9, 1992.

216. The stipulation that board members serve "in good behavior" obviously mirrors the Article III provision conferring lifetime tenure—subject to impeachment—for federal judges. That provision has worked well, insulating judges from political pressure while allowing for their removal when they become manifestly unfit.

217. *Fladell v. Palm Beach County Canvassing Board*, 772 So. 2d 1240 (Fla. 2000).

218. This consensus is described and documented by Professor Steven Mulroy in an interesting law review article, "Right Without A Remedy? The 'Butterfly Ballot' Case and Court-Ordered Federal Election 'Re-votes,'" 10 *George Mason Law Review*, 215 (2001). Professor Mulroy (who participated in the litigation challenging the butterfly ballot) takes the view that courts are already empowered to order re-votes. Even if he is right, a constitutional amendment would be needed to give PERB that power.

219. Article II, Section 1, Clause 4.

220. Julia Azari, fivethirtyeight.com/features/what-happens-if-the-election-was-a-fraud-the-constitution-doesnt-say/ July 6, 2017.

221. See Robert Reich, "If Trump Is Guilty, His Presidency Must be Annulled," *Newsweek*, February 17, 2019 (arguing that "if there's overwhelming evidence [Trump] rigged the 2016

election . . . impeachment isn't an adequate remedy. His presidency should be annulled. . . . Impeachment would not remedy Trump's unconstitutional presidency because it would leave in place his vice president, White House staff and Cabinet."). Although Reich does not specifically address what to do following his hypothetical annulment of a presidential election, a new election would clearly have to take place. One could not simply resort to the normal lines of succession, since, in Reich's hypothetical scenario, the vice president's own improper election was inseparable from the president's.

222. *Donohue v. Board of Elections of State of NY*, 435 F. Supp. 957 (E.D.N.Y. 1976). That judge held that a re-vote *is* permissible, but he did not find that fraud was demonstrated in the case at hand.

223. Dworkin, "The Phantom Toll Booth," in *A Badly Flawed Election*, 60.

224. Aazari, "What Happens If the Election Was a Fraud?," July 6, 2017, Fivethirtyeight.com.

225. Hasen, "Beyond the Margin of Litigation," 62 *Washington & Lee Law Review*, 992.

226. Dworkin, "The Phantom Toll Booth," in *A Badly Flawed Election*, 69.

227. *Hacking Elections Is Easy*, 73.

228. Posner, *Breaking the Deadlock*, 237–38.

229. Ibid., 238.